PRISMS OF LIFE

PRISMS OF LIFE

God bless you,
Lu Wayland Harkey

LU WAYLAND HARKEY

CREATION HOUSE
H O U S E
A STRANG COMPANY

Design Director: Bill Johnson
Cover design by Nathan Morgan
Illustrations by Anna Elizabeth Harkey, the author's
granddaughter.

Library of Congress Control Number: 2009939576
International Standard Book Number: 978-1-61638-005-2

First Edition

09 10 11 12 13 — 9 8 7 6 5 4 3 2 1
Printed in the United States of America

DEDICATION

To seekers who want to know that Jesus is really alive today and that He cares about you, died for you, and longs for you to seek Him. Life will never be boring.

Yours in Christ,
Lu Wayland Harkey

CONTENTS

PREFACE

THESE TRUE STORIES have been retold as a challenge to the modern mind that discounts the Bible and the historic reality of Jesus Christ. Each story is like looking through a prism in which God exists and touches the situation with His presence, wisdom, guidance, or even full intervention for His glory. In these experiences, we get a glimpse of the grace of our heavenly Father. Too often things of the Spirit are not discernable and appear as accidents or happenstance or even foolishness to the outsider. But sometimes a certain incident will open a small window and cause the reader to say, "That had to be God!" These true stories have this capability.

I dare you to ponder them.

Chapter 1
IS CINDY THERE?

BETTY PORTER WAS a striking lady with a warm personality. Many were drawn to her magnetism, expressed in caring relationships and strong faith.

The phone rang in the church office. It was Betty on the line. Peter, her husband, had dropped dead of a heart attack! Marty, her minister, rushed to offer Betty support, listening time, and prayer for strength. His guidance in making arrangements was appreciated.

Meantime, the office staff notified significant others who were glad to have the opportunity to minister to their grieving friend.

The next day, Marty returned to Betty's home to help plan the service. "What will you remember about Peter?" he asked. The grief process was beginning.

Two weeks after the memorial service, Marty called Betty and asked her if he could come by for a visit. Meeting him at the door, he was shocked at her state of despondency. After a few minutes, Marty said, "Betty, you are almost a basket case. There must be more than Peter's death. Your extreme grief is far beyond normal suffering. Can you tell me about it?"

Betty began, "Please sit down. I truly need your help. Not only have I buried my second husband, but also years ago, I lost my only child—a daughter, age sixteen. I guess Peter's death has brought back all my old grief. Her name was Cindy, and her death was recorded in official files as a suicide. If she did take her life I will never see her again!

"She was a precious girl—popular cheerleader, good grades, a professed faith in the living Lord. In fact, her father and I could not think of any reason she would want to die. Yet the evidence stood. The garage door was shut, the car door was open, the motor was running, and Cindy was lying on the floor dead. I know that I will see her father again. I know that I will see Peter again. I can't stand the thought that I will never be with Cindy."

Silence held the air captive for a few moments.

Marty spoke, "Who told you that you would not see Cindy again?"

"At the time, I was a member of a church whose leadership said that suicide is an unforgivable sin."

Marty opened his Bible to Matthew 12:31 and read the following words: "Anyone who speaks a word against the Son of Man will be forgiven, but anyone who speaks against the Holy Spirit will not be forgiven, either in this age or in the age to come" (NIV).

Marty continued, "There is no reference in Scripture to any other unforgivable sin. The Holy Spirit is the Illuminator, the one who reveals unto us that Jesus is truly God in the flesh. If in full knowledge, we blaspheme the Spirit by rejecting Jesus Christ as our Savior and Lord, we commit the unforgivable sin."

Marty then read Romans 8:38 and 39: "For I am convinced that neither death nor life, neither angels nor demons, neither the present nor the future, nor any powers, neither height nor depth, nor anything else in all creation, will be able to separate us from the love of God that is in Christ Jesus our Lord" (NIV).

"Betty, why do you think that God had Paul list the word *death* first?" There was a pause in the conversation. Marty continued, "I believe it was recorded because we think of death as being final, and we feel the physical separation intensely. Death in any form cannot separate us from God's love in Jesus Christ."

After several meetings, Marty realized that Betty still did not have the measure of peace concerning Cindy that would bring joy to her life. He prayed about the matter and decided to suggest a thirty-day prayer covenant: they would both pray daily for God to somehow show her the truth and give her His peace. She agreed.

A week later, Betty phoned to share that she had received word from her sister who lived near Chicago that her mother had a limited time to live. Her mother wanted to come home from the assisted care facility and die in the old home place where the sister now lived. The sister who called said, "If you will come and help us, we can handle around-the-clock care." A second sister from California was on her way to join the team.

Betty explained she needed to end the conversation because the airport limousine was due. She promised to keep in touch and continue the prayer covenant with Marty.

In a little over two weeks, Betty returned to her home in Treasure Island, Florida. Excited, she called Marty to share how God had answered their prayers.

One afternoon while sitting with her quietly sleeping mom, she noticed her mother's breathing was gradually slowing down, until her breath was gone. Betty said, "She bowed her head and thanked God she had gone peacefully to be with Him." After what seemed like several minutes, her mother gasped for breath and began breathing again. She returned to total consciousness, expressing real excitement. Betty called one of her sisters, who was in another part of the house. They listened as their mother spoke.

"It was like a curtain was rolled back. I saw all our loved ones

3

we have lost." She named her parents and several others. "They are all there waiting for me. I saw them!"

Breathlessly Betty asked, "Cindy? Mom, did you see Cindy? Was she there?"

"Yes! She is there; I saw her! She is with the others!"

She shared more and then, lying back on her pillow, expressed how tired she felt. Peacefully, she was allowed to fall asleep again.

After a brief period, again her breathing became irregular, slowed, and stopped. This time there was no return. God had answered Betty's prayer in a wonderful way. Her joy was too great for human expression. Now she would be able to move on with her life, her heavy burden lifted. Her heart was filled with peace and praise to the almighty God who cares for each of us.

> Casting the whole of your care [all your anxieties, all your worries, all your concerns, once and for all] on Him, for He cares for you affectionately and cares about you watchfully.
>
> —1 PETER 5:7

Chapter 2
BEAUTIFUL MAN

T WO OF US were invited, as Stephen's Ministers, to serve as assistant chaplains at the ostomy wing of a major hospital in Florida. The time was in the mid eighties. For identification, we wore badges clearly inscribed with lettering large enough to be read by the patients.

One day a week we each visited post-operative patients who desired our company. Following their surgeries, we gave them several days to begin to heal before our first visit. Many of the patients—most under forty, young adults—were from different parts of the United States. Because of the excellent surgery being done at this time, they traveled the distance required to come to this hospital. For some patients, a family member made the trip. Others were alone. The length of stay was customarily six weeks. As they began to heal, many desired sensitive, responsive listeners. We were trained to meet this need.

Visitation time for me took place on Monday. The first room I approached was marked by five-inch letters posted over the door that read International Precaution, which signaled the patient inside had AIDS. (The medical profession knew little about help for AIDS patients at the time.)

I stepped to the closest nursing station, I was given clearance to visit, accompanied by a word of caution: "Don't touch the patient, and wash your hands before you enter another room."

Knocking, I read the name of the patient, which was secured in the brass frame to the left of the door. I'll call him Lynn.

I heard, "Come in."

Turning the knob, I froze as I noticed the handsome man laying on the hospital bed—totally nude!

Obviously making my exit, I said, "I'll be back at a more convenient time."

"No, please don't go. I want you to pray for me."

I stepped back inside of the room and bowed my head, thinking, "Lord, what do I pray?" These words came: "Lord, would You make Lynn as beautiful inside as he is outside? In Jesus' name I pray, amen."

Lynn responded in surprise with the realization of an exciting new direction for his life.

The next week, we left town on a study leave and vacation. When we returned to the city and the hospital rounds, Lynn's room was occupied by another patient.

Time elapsed.

Again, I moved about the ostomy wing.

Deliberately, I skipped a room where a doctor was in conference with the patient.

I heard a voice call out, "Hey, Lu!"

Walking closer to the room, I saw Lynn in a chair, peering around the doctor. His face was thin, his color was not good, but his eyes reflected a spirit at peace.

He called to me, "Just wanted you to know, it is up to the Lord now!"

We are told of the lasting beauty of the inner self, "a gentle and quiet spirit, which is so precious to the Lord" (1 Pet. 3:4, NLT).

Like Shadrach, Meshach, and Abednego in the lions' den, Lynn can say:

> God whom we serve is able...but if He does not deliver us...yet will we trust Him.
>
> —DANIEL 3:17–18, AUTHOR'S PARAPHRASE

Chapter 3
NOAH'S ARK

S HE WAS AN old barn converted into a used book depository—
two sizable floors and not an empty shelf. Many an elderly
person had cleared out their private libraries and attics to make
up her contents. Some families, distributing their received inheri-
tance, chose to ship their old books to this barn for whatever they
would bring in the marketplace. Other folk who enjoyed old books
drove great distances in order to read the titles of these treasures
and purchase what their budgets could handle.

She was located in the historic town of Abbeville, South Carolina. Just because I enjoy older things—books, handmade lace, and
antiques—I drove my car the twenty-one miles from where I lived
in Anderson, South Carolina, to where she could be found.

Twenty-one years earlier, when my husband was a student at the
University of Virginia, he was struggling with Unitarian thought.
He longed to know more about the divinity of Christ. My dad, a
pastor, recommended a tiny, out-of-print book entitled *The Deity
of Christ*, written by Dr. Robert E. Speer. A copy was located at
the Union Seminary Library in Richmond, Virginia. It was the
resource needed to answer his questions. Because the book had
helped him, I tossed a flash prayer to the Lord: "Lord, lead us to

a copy of this book for our library so that others may be blessed."
Years went by and that prayer remained unanswered.

On this day, as I crossed the threshold of Noah's Ark for the
first time, into my mind came the thought, "Your book is here!"
Accompanying the word of knowledge, I knew which book it was!
I glanced at the shelves on the first floor with no desire to look
further in that area. I climbed the stairs as if I were being gently
led. From the top step, my eyes fell on five small books. I was
filled with excitement as I approached these books. The fifth book
I examined was my book! I was in awe of what was taking place. I
could hardly believe it. The price delighted me, and it was in good
condition, too!

Our Lord had not forgotten the flash prayer after all those years.
I had not remembered it. Since that day, He has used the little
book with Catholics and Protestants as He did with Marty.

I believe our precious Lord enjoyed this experience, as did I.

Great is the Lord, and highly to be praised!

—PSALM 48:1

Chapter 4
FORGET YOUR LITTLE GIRL!

IT WAS THE eve of Thanksgiving. Rosanne, two years and four months old, was the only daughter and granddaughter in two families. With trepidation, we left her in the intensive care unit of our city's children's hospital.

As Rosanne awoke earlier that morning, I had heard her call out, "Mommy." There was something different about the call. It was filled with fear. From the kitchen, I rushed to her room. Rosanne was standing, but her legs were unsteady. Both eyes looked strange, and her face was flushed. I called my five-year-old son, Luke, and asked him to bring the thermometer, directing him to the top drawer in the blue bathroom.

Rapidly, he was at my side with the thermometer in hand. Placing my left hand under my daughter, I laid her down. My right hand held steady the glass temperature measure. I knew before I read the thermometer we were looking at a fever close to being out of control.

I phoned a neighbor and got no answer. Another neighbor was seen walking into her backyard with her baby in her arms. I sent Luke to get her; I needed help! The neighbor speedily came with her preschool-aged son trailing behind. She would be glad to stay with all four kids, she said. At the time, our younger son, Wayland, was seven months old. Our neighbor's baby was a little younger.

I grabbed my coat as my friend called the family pediatrician. By the time I reached the doctor's office, I was carrying Rosanne, who by then could not take a step. Her temperature had continued to climb. One glance at Rosanne and the nurse ran for the doctor. He came into the room followed by a second nurse. It was frightening to look at her. A nurse attempted to draw blood. She could not get the needle into her small, rolling blood vessels.

Usually calm, happy, and cooperative, Rosanne was crying hysterically. It took all four adults to restrain her so that her arms and legs remained still. With calm patience from the team and the assurances of Mom's voice, the procedure was finally successful and vials were ready for the laboratory.

The doctor spoke, "Let's get her to the hospital immediately!" He asked a nurse to locate my husband, Marty, through his office and ask him to please come without hesitation.

On our arrival at the hospital, a laboratory technician was called and a culture was taken. The doctor and I stayed quietly at the side of the bed where Rosanne had been placed.

Marty rushed into the room out of breath. "Tell me what is going on!"

The doctor spoke, "We do not know what is wrong. We hope we will know when the culture grows and we can study the results." We sat quietly; after a period of time the doctor spoke, "Seeing your child in this condition has to be traumatic for both of you. Why don't you take a break and get a bite of lunch? I will not leave her."

We knew the fever was still rising and an extended high fever over a long period of time could cook her brain. The situation was dangerous, and we felt helpless.

We needed time to think. In a daze, we nibbled on a couple sandwiches, pushed our salads away, and left. Our parents needed to be told what was happening, and our church must be called to prayer.

As we walked down the corridor toward Rosanne's room, our doctor met us in the hall.

"I cannot offer you any encouragement. It does not look good. Go home; I will call you if there is any change. She would not know you now."

Reluctantly, we obliged. Hours passed. No word meant she was still alive.

The next day, the doctor called. The culture had not grown as anticipated. Prayers continued to ascend to our heavenly Father.

"Lord, please make the culture grow. Lord, if she could bless You and others, please choose life."

Sleep escaped Marty and me. We could think only of our sick little girl. At the end of forty-eight hours, the doctor called. "The culture has grown, and the diagnosis is bacterial spinal meningitis. The only treatment available today that sometimes can kill the bacteria is in the family of the sulfur drugs. We are administering the sulfur, but this is a virulent case. Try to forget you have a little girl; if she lives, she will have to exist in an institution. No human brain could survive the height of temperature she has already endured for this extended period of time. We have not been successful in lowering it a single degree."

"May we see her?"

"I don't think it would be wise. She is in isolation and too sick to recognize you."

More time lapsed. Seven days passed with no change.

Julia, our friend, helped me two days a week while my husband traveled.

She shared her grief. "I feel responsible for Rosanne's illness! When I was sick nearly three weeks ago, you came to my home to bring food and money for my drugs. I believe I had the same serious illness that Rosanne suffers today. Big as I am, I almost died. Remember that even though you had a friend in the car with the children, Rosanne got out of the car and broke for my house. We were both horrified when she ran into my room and kissed me. But don't you worry, honey. I'm president of my church's women's ministry, and I have rallied over a thousand ladies for prayer on her behalf."

Many others called us to say they were praying for God's will in the matter. Our home was permeated with peace beyond anything we had previously known. Caring people continued to call. I answered the phone so many times my voice became hoarse. There was so much peace that we became willing to release Rosanne to the Lord.

Under the shade of the carefully planted Chinaberry tree, Wayland watched from his stroller and observed Luke at play. I sat under the same tree and stitched a garment for Rosanne. It helped.

Marty's mom, who lived a short distance away, parked her car in our driveway. As she came toward me and realized what I was doing, she spoke to me.

"Lu, put that garment down; you are torturing yourself."

She was speaking from experience. She and her husband, whom we called Dad Luke, had lost their only daughter with whooping cough at thirteen months of age.

I remember saying, "If our precious Rosanne cannot wear this jumper, I'll find a child that it fits and give it to her."

Marty's dad called to tell us that a Shriner friend had died of bacterial spinal meningitis, and his wife said of him, "His dying words were, 'Is the Harkey baby going to make it?'"

I remember saying to Marty's dad, "You know, Dad Luke, Marty and I thank God for giving us such a lovely little girl for two years and four months. We know that each of the children is on loan from God, and their times, as well as ours, are in His hands. He gives us freedom, which Rosanne took when she kissed a very sick woman on her mouth." (Previously we had never observed her kiss anyone on the mouth!)

Suddenly, on the eleventh day, the fever broke! She began to improve rapidly.

We were excited! On the fourteenth day, we were told she could go home. We were full of joy and ready to leave for the hospital. As we walked toward the door, the phone began to ring. Rosanne's fever had spiked again, and she could not be released. We thought meningitis had again reared its ugly head. We later learned the new fever was not connected to meningitis. She had picked up a virus from another child whose room she had visited.

Three days more brought her homecoming. Her eyes would cross as she tired and headaches occurred for several years. Regular appointments with an ophthalmologist took place over the next five years. This amounted to nothing—she was alive and seemed normal.

Our hearts were full of praise to God!

Our pediatrician, who had been faithful through Rosanne's illness, had suggested that we wait until she was of school age to have her intellect tested.

A year later, her two-day-a-week playschool teacher called to me as I was in the line of cars to pick up kids in my carpool. "Park your car and I'll send someone to sit with the kids for a short time. I want to show you something!"

As we walked toward her room, she told me many of the teachers had gotten a big kick out of a picture Rosanne had drawn. The children were given pencil and paper and told to draw a picture of something happening in their home every day. (I had told her teachers earlier of Rosanne's narrow brush with death, days of extremely high fever, and asked her if she would let me know her personal evaluation of her mind as the school year rolled past.)

She turned the picture over and handed it to me. Rosanne had drawn a comical picture of her dad—his head, eyes, brows, ears, nose, mouth, torso, and all four limbs, with ten fingers and ten toes.

We rejoiced! She would be able to be a contributor to the world in His name.

The Christmas following her illness, Rosanne asked for a nurse's uniform. Dad and I believe her choice of vocation goes back to her seventeen days at the hospital and the loving care of nurses and doctors.

Today she holds a PhD in nursing and is a university professor.

Glory to God and God's blessing on all medical personnel who are diligent in their calling and truly care about others!

Serve the Lord with gladness.

—PSALM 100:2

Whoever wishes to be great among you must be your servant.

—MATTHEW 20:26

Chapter 5
GOD HAD A WORD FOR ME

MARTY, AN ELECTRICAL engineer with General Electric Company, was transferred to the State of Florida by his division regional manager. We were leaving the Carolinas and a wonderful support system of four grandparents, a sister, brother and wife, and many friends.

Luke, our oldest son, had his sixth birthday less than a week before the moving van arrived. His sister, Rosanne, had her third birthday the same week. Our younger son, Wayland, was seventeen months old.

Rosanne was still experiencing severe headaches, vision problems, and other consequences from her recent case with bacterial spinal meningitis.

Marty flew south to scout possible places we might live in the area of Tampa Bay. During a phone conversation, we made the decision to find a home in St. Petersburg. The beach, soft breezes, and sunshine would be a blessing to our allergy-prone kids.

Marty phoned, "Safely place the children and fly down. We will make the home decision together."

We bought a home under construction and were allowed to make plan changes to suit our taste. The house was several months from completion date. This would necessitate a further search for temporary housing. To fill this bill was no small task. Finally, we found a small rental house located on a tiny, unfenced piece of property. At the time it seemed to be the only place available.

We both returned home, and I flew down to St. Pete with the three kids to meet the moving van. Marty stayed in the Carolinas to train his replacement engineer.

August heat in Florida was very warm; air conditioning was uncommon. I opened all the steel casement windows and realized there was no cross ventilation. The proximity of other houses blocked the breeze. I could not use a fan, since the two younger children might put their fingers into the works. (In those days fans with protective frames were not available.) Allowing kids to play in the unfenced yard would be unsafe. Since we were temporary renters, we could not install a fence.

Days passed. Luke tried to entertain the other children. It was difficult; most of his toys and books were packed in boxes under boxes. He was accustomed to having many children on the block who frequented his yard. No kids were around. We had selected a retirement area! You might ask, Why did you not take the children to one of the city's excellent parks, where the kids would be playing? Doctors orders. "Don't take Rosanne into groups until her immune system has had time to strengthen!"

The children did not readily acclimate to the late summer change from milder weather to hot weather. The kids were energetic, but with no outlet for their energy, the two younger ones began to cry excessively in an irritating manner. I knew it must bother the neighbors. This was confirmed by a screaming voice exclaiming, "Shut those kids up! Stuff rags in their mouths!"

I cringed! (Later, when our house was ready and we were moving, several neighbors came over to apologize for the man's behavior. I learned he was an alcoholic.)

Finally, I was at wit's end. I piled all three youngsters and our small dog in my car, which GE had shipped for me. I did not know where I would go. I knew no one in the city. I drove and drove. With the windows open, the children relaxed in the cooler air and change of scenery.

Though normally even tempered, I was far from calm as I began to silently pray as I drove, "Lord, I don't want to upset family or friends by calling home. Marty is not available. The children sense the confusion and frustration of the situation. You and I both know I have to get away from these kids for an hour to maintain my sanity."

I continued to drive. Impressed on my mind was the following thought: "Watch for the next bus stop. There will be a woman waiting there. Ask her if she will work for you one day a week."

In my mind a heavy question arose: Should I ask someone I knew nothing about to help me ? Suppose this was not the Lord speaking to me. I prayed, "Lord, is this You, or is my imagination playing games? Lord, at this time of day there could be many people waiting for the bus. If this is You, would you confirm this word given?"

The next bus stop came into view. Alone at the stop stood a lady! Edging my car to the curb, I got out and walked toward her to look her over. Drawing close to her, I was touched by her expression of kindness. I noted she was watching all the activity in my car! (Confirmation?)

I dared to speak. "We are newcomers to the city. My husband will be traveling most weeks. I need a person who loves kids to help me one day a week."

"I am that person! Today was my last day of work for an elderly man whose family will be moving him to an assisted care facility. I was wondering what I would do to fill my work week."

After several weeks of observing the dynamics of this lady with our children, I felt free to leave in order to purchase groceries and have a few minutes alone. This wonderful woman blessed our lives for the next five years we lived in St. Pete. She was like an angel. God cares!

Looking back many years later, I realized God had given me a gift of knowledge. Are you aware when He intervenes in your life?

The Lord shall guide you continually.

—ISAIAH 58:11

Chapter 6
AN UNEXPECTED RESPONSE

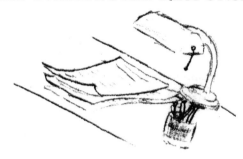

THE INVITATION ARRIVED. "Will you serve on the admissions committee of your alma mater?"

One weekend in the fall would be spent in a preparatory workshop. The college would cover my flight expenses. I would also represent the school on college night at local high schools in the St. Pete and Tampa area. They would count on me for any requested follow-up.

The weekend arrived. I began to meet the other alumni with whom I would serve. Beautifully groomed, the young women appeared to be very bright and successfully making their mark on the world.

Everything was well planned.

As the work sessions progressed, much was accomplished. In order to reach our goals, it was announced that we would work through Sunday morning.

I was not enthused but felt that I should say nothing. It was 11:15 a.m. on Sunday. We were working steadily. One member of our team spoke. "Where are the sixteen prospective students who were visiting the campus yesterday?

As they made plans to attend church, I had overheard their

conversation. I paused a second in my work and in kindness answered, "They are in church."

As we broke for lunch, a young alumna from the Midwest came up to me. "We were told that you were a clergy wife, and we expected you to preach to us for cutting church. We were ready to counter any argument that you might give us. You made no response. I posed the question about the students on purpose. I knew that you had overheard their plans because you were standing near them. There was something about the way you said, 'They are in church,' that reminded me I have not been in church in ten years. I am starting back next Sunday."

Jesus was never pushy. He loved unconditionally, as does His Father, and along the way one after another chose to follow His example.

> Those who are led by the Spirit of God are sons of God....The Spirit Himself testifies with our spirit that we are God's children.
>
> —ROMANS 8:14, 16, NIV

Chapter 7
GOD'S TIMING

For the previous thirteen years, the General Electric company had employed my husband as an electrical engineer. He was a thirty-four-year-old only child. His decision to answer a call to enter seminary and the ministry had upset his dad, who had other plans for his son's future. His dad said in extreme anger, "If you make this move, I will disinherit you!"

Marty told his dad, "I love you, and I have always listened to you, but this time I must be obedient to my heavenly Father."

Knowing his dad, Marty realized this wasn't a time for further discussion. He picked up his bag, hugged his Mom, and walked to the rental car. He was pensive as he drove to the airport and boarded the plane for our Florida home.

Arriving at home, he told me the trip was the toughest flight that he had ever made. He was torn because of his father's reaction to this difficult decision.

Our immediate prayer was, "Lord, would you confirm this call in two weeks' time by selling our house and the boat for the amount we have in them?" (We knew that McDill Field in Tampa had temporarily closed and the houses of many of their employees flooded our market.) It was late June 1960, and our window for action was narrow. We had to decide on a seminary, gain acceptance, find a place to live, and move before school opened for the kids. This prayer required a miracle, and God answered it in the affirmative. In order to pay off our church pledge, we signed over our second car to the church for a staff employee.

Marty had promised his regional manager at General Electric to make the transition as smooth as possible with a number of substantial customers. He would train his replacement engineer. The word given him was in the affirmative.

Entertaining much anxiety, we moved into a two-bedroom apartment with a promise for a third bedroom in one year. The school was Columbia Theological Seminary in Decatur, Georgia. Luke was ready for sixth grade, Rosanne was preparing to enter the third grade, and Wayland was excited about beginning real school.

All went well. I moved with the children in August; Marty would follow in late September. I applied to teach school. Before this could be processed, we got a call from Marty's dad. His minister had convinced him he should thank God for putting His hand on his son. "Get behind him and make his journey easier," he told him. Dad Luke had listened and prayed.

He said, "If Lu will be available for those three grandchildren, I will pay her a teacher's salary." (In the area, a teacher with two years' experience teaching in a high school would draw six thousand dollars.) His message was wonderful. We thanked him profusely. Now I could type and edit papers, be a classroom mom, den mother, Bluebird leader, and be available when needed by Marty and other student wives.

One problem still existed. Marty did not want me to spend any money on clothing. By leaving General Electric after thirteen years instead of fifteen, he lost his retirement and all medical coverage. Luke needed a warmer jacket for the cooler climate. Marty insisted our savings were to be for emergency only! I prayed, "Lord, Luke's leather jacket is new, but it is unlined. He needs a size 14 with a fleece lining like the other kids his age are wearing. If you will find him one, I'll give you his jacket for a kid moving to a warmer climate." I told no one about my prayer.

Two weeks later, a professor's wife, Mrs. Manford Gutzke, called me and said, "Lu, a leather jacket was just brought to my door. I know it is for Luke." I rapidly walked to her nearby home.

When she came to the door with the jacket, my eyes were looking at the exact jacket for which I had prayed: nearly new brown leather, size 14, with sheepskin fleece lining!

Note the orchestration: God had to plant the thought in a person's mind who had a jacket and didn't need it. The person had to be willing to release the jacket and have knowledge as to whom she should take it. Mrs. Gutzke had to be listening to the Lord to call me.

As I thanked Mrs. Gutzke, I told her about my prayer. Together we rejoiced!

"There were several boys Luke's size living in the village and around campus. Had she noticed his light jacket?" I asked.

"No, she said God had told her in her spirit to give it to Luke."

I ran to our apartment and sent Luke to thank her and take her his unlined leather jacket to be shared. My prayer asked God to bless each one involved.

Marty was in shock when I told him of the experience. He thought God was teaching us to trust Him in all circumstances. We thought the decision to go to seminary meant poverty vows, and God was telling us He owned the cattle on a thousand hills.

Lord, we have much to learn from You, the Master Teacher.

What time I am afraid, I will have confidence in and put my trust and reliance in You. By [the help of] God I will praise His word; on God I lean, rely, and confidently put my trust; I will not fear. What can man, who is flesh, do to me?

—PSALM 56:3–4

Chapter 8
LET ME LOVE HER THROUGH YOUR EYES

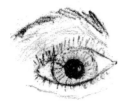

I LOST PATIENCE WITH her. Saying nothing, I tried to avoid her. She was present at a gathering of nearly sixty women brought together to face important problems and seek positive solutions.

She had come from the middle of our nation, where many great people live, but somewhere, at some time, she had stood alone to defend herself. She was irritating and hurtful to those around her.

In my spirit, I judged her. I knew it was the wrong attitude to take, yet I could not escape it.

Then the Master Teacher interrupted my thoughts. "You could never imagine what this young lady has endured! All this week I want you to let Me love her through your eyes."

"Lord, I do not have any idea how to unpack your request. Guide me and fill me afresh with your Spirit; I feel drained."

It was as though He drew me to her. I sought her out and acted as if I had not been aware of her negative actions. When she said something to me, I listened, not judging her comments. This happened several times.

When we had small tasks to accomplish, I asked her to work with me. If she was trying to do something well, I congratulated her on the accomplishment.

I remember, on one occasion I slipped my arm around her. I truly began to care for her.

On the seventh day, she threw her arms around me. I was surprised to hear her say thank you.

"Why do you thank me? I have done nothing worthy of thanks."

"You have freed me."

"What do you mean?"

"I was ignored or given back what I dished out. You loved me. All the anger is gone!"

Lord, continue teaching me Your ways.

> Sometimes God calms the storm. Sometimes He calms the child and lets the storm rage on.
>
> —ANONYMOUS

> Show me Your ways, O Lord; teach me Your paths.
>
> —PSALM 25:4

Chapter 9
A SENSE OF FAIRNESS

NINETEEN SIXTY-EIGHT ARRIVED. Our elder son, a Duke University freshman, taught a course in life-saving for students who wanted credit for this venture. He enjoyed his Martin guitar. His love of people helped him make the decision to join a fraternity. The fraternity he chose was made up of students who possessed, as a part of their character, sensitive social consciences and a sense of right and wrong.

Home for the weekend, he handed his father an article from the *Washington Post*. The article reported, "Many students assembled in Washington from a number of colleges and universities to say a strong word to the Coca-Cola Company. The word: There are people who need jobs; hire those of different color as well as Caucasians!" The writer continued his report by stating the only visible destruction was of a Coca-Cola stand. We asked Luke to tell us about the weekend.

"My fraternity decided this was an issue on which we wanted to take a positive stand; we decided to make the trip to Washington. We were nearby when some other students destroyed the stand. I grabbed the cash register and took it to the nearest store that sold Coke." (His mom and dad's reaction: "You could have been jailed for stealing!")

Luke continued, "I told the manager, 'This belongs to the Coca-Cola Company; will you see that they get it?'" Our fraternity gathered enough money to cover the cost of the destroyed Coke stand. I took it to the same store where I had left the cash register. I asked them to put the additional money with the register for the Coca-Cola Company. He assured me he would comply."

His dad and I caught our breath as Marty read the last sentence of the *Post* article out loud. "There was a tall, lanky young man moving among the students doing good. I asked his name. His answer was, 'I'm nameless.'"

The next summer, this same young man was attending a youth conference of young people from all over the Southeast. He walked into the lobby of the main assembly building as teens of color were confronted by a gang of white teens who had just sliced their displayed drawings. The black youth had asked them to stop, and they had refused. Tempers were flaring, and knives were being lifted. This young man stood between the two groups and in God's love asked questions and listened until the situation calmed down. The white boys (who were not a part of the conference or from the area) got in their cars and left the premises, taking their knives with them. He put the black boys in his car and took them to the dorms where they were housed.

A company manager hired him the following summer from mid-June to September. He worked with a polished black student. He noticed that his fellow worker was not getting a restroom break, as he was being given. He said to him, "The next time I get a break, you go and I will work." Luke was caught and received verbal abuse.

At the end of the day, the supervisor, who was very angry, went to the manager and owner of the franchise. He told him all about what Luke had done.

The manager told the supervisor he was wrong for not allowing the black employee a break, as he had given Luke! The manager reached for the phone and called Luke's dad. "Thank you for your son's courage!" he said. "I had no idea any of my workers were receiving such treatment. Change has taken place thanks to your son."

> For I have known (chosen, acknowledged) him [as My own], so that he may teach and command his children and the sons of his house after him to keep the way of the Lord and to do what is just and righteous.
>
> —GENESIS 18:19

Chapter 10
HOLD THE PHONE

THE AMERICAN KENNEL Association would not have approved of the rating that we gave our dog. Yet, all three kids agreed that they had grounds for it. After all, her mom, a Dachshund, and her dad, a Chihuahua, were both pedigreed neighbors. Two pedigrees make a double, don't they?

Chip was chosen from the litter, no question. An alert, active black ball who left her siblings to check out our kids, she belonged with our crew. As she developed, her legs grew just a little longer and her nose stopped short of her dad's. Her cigar-shaped body and people-loving personality were copies of her mom. She had sensitive ears that brought forth a bark to warn us when someone was approaching the house. Who needed a doorbell with Chip around?

She took turns sleeping with the kids. They loved her and could hardly wait their turn.

Our youngest son, a rising third grader who was visiting out-of-state grandparents for the first time alone, wrote the following question in a note to me: "How are Chip and Dad?" (in that order).

Her only trick was "dead dog." My husband enjoyed needling his two pastor friends, who lived in our neighborhood. He asked Chip, in their presence, if she would rather be a pastor of the friend's denomination or a dead dog. On cue, she would drop to the floor and remain in a freeze until released. Then she would move close to the visitors as if to say, "Forgive me!"

At the manse, her sensitivity to people was evident. If a person came who needed to talk, she would sit at attention and keep her eyes glued on the speaker, and then she would turn to me to see how I would respond. When there was prayer, she closed her eyes. If there were tears, she snuggled to the distressed visitor.

In her old age, she had experienced surgery and was irritated by repetitive noise. She was forced to make an adjustment.

A good friend, Carolyn, in passing said, "Lu, something is wrong at your house! I dialed your phone number and all I got was deep breathing." She is the only person that I remember commenting on the subject. If another friend spoke to me about the matter, I did not take it seriously. Feeling at peace in myself, I could not hear their concern. Our children were all away in college. Marty and I were the only ones living in the manse. I had not read anything suspicious in his behavior, and I knew that I was sane! My response was flippant. Upset, she left me.

After a period of time, Marty began to complain, "Would you please replace the telephone receiver on the hook when you finish a phone call?"

I responded, "I do that automatically."

Later he approached the subject again, "I can never reach you."

"I am not guilty," I insisted.

One day the phone rang as Marty opened the back door.

Someone answered it. Since I was teaching school, he knew that no one was supposed to be in the house. He could see the kitchen phone, and looking down the hall, he observed the hall phone. Only the bedroom phone was not visible. He tiptoed down the hall and looked in the bedroom door to see the remaining phone. There was Chip, standing on the bed, with the receiver in her mouth. Marty, with keen hearing, could hear a voice saying, "Hello." Chip dropped the receiver and was sniffing the source of the voice.

Later we set it up. I would dial our number from the church. Marty would quietly observe Chip's action through the lens of a camera. He would record the event.

The next Sunday, carrying the snapshot, he entered the pulpit.

"We owe you, the congregation, an explanation," he began. "We understand that you have been calling the manse and getting a seductive response. We now have the answer. Our dog has been answering the phone, dropping the receiver, and breathing into it for the source of the voice. You may examine the picture after the service."

As laughter broke out in the sanctuary, a friend seated next to me said, "I've known for six months that something was wrong, and I have not said a word to a person."

Marty's voice was heard again, "We are here to worship the Lord and give thanks."

> And the Lord opened the mouth of the donkey, and she said to Balaam, What have I done to you that you should strike me these three times? And Balaam said to the donkey, Because you have ridiculed and provoked me!
>
> —NUMBERS 22:28–29

Chapter 11
KATHY

A Word of Background

FOR TWENTY-FIVE YEARS, I have known I was to write Kathy's story. I was reluctant to begin; it was not my story, but Kathy's. After fourteen years of residence in another state, we moved back into the area where Kathy and her husband, David, live with their two sons, David and Daniel.

One morning, I felt God was nudging me to write all I could recall of this story. Then the phone rang. It was Kathy.

"Lu, will you write my story? God has given me another miracle, and I want my husband to know about the one that occurred when I was a little girl."

Kathy, here is your story.

> My little daughter is at the point of death. Come and lay
> your hands on her, so that she may be healed and live.
> And Jesus went with him....Little girl, I say to you, arise
> [from the sleep of death]! And instantly, the girl got up
> and started around—for she was twelve years old."
> —MARK 5:23–24, 41–42

Jesus Christ (the Messiah) is [always] the same, yesterday, today, [yes] and forever (to the ages).

—HEBREWS 13:8

Dick Anderson rushed to his car, put his keys in the ignition, revved the motor, stepped on the gas, and drove and drove and drove—and screamed at God!

Grief, frustration, anger, and the helpless inability to control the situation, were the emotions that rose to the surface of the young father. It was difficult to accept the doctor's diagnosis that had been given to him and his lovely wife, Elsie. Their two-year-old daughter was the victim of a rare bone cancer. From this kind of cancer, only 3 percent survived, and these were unexplained.

During a routine shampoo, Elsie had discovered a soft spot on her little girl's scalp. She was active, and it was normal to believe she had experienced the bump as the result of a toddler tumble. Elsie took no action. Weeks later, the soft spot was still there. It was not natural for a child past her second birthday. There was no fever.

Elsie felt foolish when she called their excellent pediatrician. He examined Kathy and sent her to the Anderson Hospital for a culture. They were expecting to find a treatable infection, but the results did not encourage them. She was referred to a team of specialists who studied the biopsy and verified that it was a rare bone malignancy.

It was 1968. My husband, Marty, was the new pastor at the church where the Anderson family were active members. The counseling load was extremely heavy. Along with sermon preparations and the normal work of a minister, he was learning the names of officers and many members. He had heard the Andersons had a very sick little girl. Planning to go to their home but feeling helpless, he buried the thought.

After four and one-half months of carrying the burdens of others and experiencing difficulty releasing the weight to our heavenly Father, Marty decided to attend a work session at the Pastoral Counseling Institute near Athens, Georgia. This institute brought together medical doctors who were working for a doctorate in psychiatry, ministers, and troubled clients. Great problem-solving took place as a result of the intense dialogue.

The participants were housed in dorm rooms with six bunks to a room. It was dark when Marty, resting in his bunk, saw a vision! With his logical mind—trained first as an electrical engineer and employed by a nationally recognized company—he had no room in his thinking for such an occurrence. Could he be losing his mind?

He said, "It was like looking at a television screen without a box housing it." It was a picture of a young couple and a little girl. He saw himself in the picture praying for the child. He recognized the faces of Dick and Elsie and assumed that the little girl was their daughter. In his spirit, he knew that he was being told to lay hands on the child for healing. His hands felt charged with high voltage electricity.

"Lord, if this is You, You have the wrong person. I am a mainstream minister, and we don't do that kind of thing. In fact, we were taught in the seminary that miracles ceased with the death of the apostles." The vision remained constant.

"Lord, I have never seen this child, and I don't even know her name! Lord, if this is of You, give me her name." As though written in red neon across the vision, there appeared the name Kathy, and then the vision vanished.

He lay in his bunk for a short time. Lying there listening to the snore of another bunk occupant, he pinched himself. There was no question he was awake. Fear gripped him. He reached for his flashlight, got up, pulled on his trousers, and made his way to the door of the room. There was a church directory in his car! He opened the glove compartment and reached for the directory.

There was the listing: "Dick and Elsie Anderson, Rick and Mary Katherine." God had used the intimate name Kathy! The remainder of the night he tossed in his bunk as he struggled with the experience. This was new territory for him.

Early the next morning, he made a phone call to Dr. William Crane, who was the director at the institute, saying, "I need to talk to you!" Dr. Crane, sensing Marty's distress, gave him an appointment that afternoon.

Marty arrived early. Dr. Crane joined him on the porch swing. He asked Marty, "What is on your mind?"

His experience of the previous night was poured forth. "Dr. Crane, refer me to a place where I can receive some counseling."

"Marty, you are not the first person who has come to me with a story of God's intervention in their lives," Dr. Crane responded. "Our heavenly Father has given you a mandate. You can choose to obey Him or ignore His request. I think He is trying to teach you something."

Marty was not due at home for another day. When he arrived, he said, "Let's talk," as he opened the back door.

As he finished sharing, my response was, "Let's go."

"You don't help a bit," he exclaimed. "I don't know my officers well enough to know how they would handle this kind of situation. They might tar and feather me and run us out of town."

Soon Marty picked up the phone and dialed the Andersons. Marty asked Elsie about their little girl and then asked, "What do you call her?"

"She was baptized Mary Katherine, and the family calls her Kathy."

Because Kathy's grandfather, Hampton Sr., was an active elder in the church, Marty felt the need to ask his permission. We met at his home at ten the following morning. Marty shared the vision and then said, "If this is of me, nothing will happen, and it could damage the faith of Dick and Elsie. If it truly is of God, you can see the implication."

The grandfather said, "We have no choice. This child is dying. She has been given two months to live." He then phoned Dick at work and told him to go home. "Reverend Harkey will meet you there in half an hour. You need to hear what he has to say."

We drove to the home of Dick and Elsie. As soon as we were seated, Marty spoke. "If what I have to tell you is of me, some psychological projection, nothing will happen. If this is of God, He plans to move on behalf of Kathy." He then shared his experience.

Elsie began to cry softly. She spoke with deep feeling, "I've always felt that God would intervene."

Kathy had a splendid local doctor who worked with an exceptionally fine oncologist at the medical college of the University of Virginia (Marty's undergraduate alma mater).

Dick, Elsie, and Kathy were to leave early Sunday morning for their monthly appointment at the medical school. All agreed Saturday evening was the time for prayer. We arrived at seven and saw Kathy for the first time. She ran to Marty and gave him a big hug. When we were seated, she climbed on his lap and asked him to take her out under the stars. It was a cold evening in February. Elsie bundled her up. Marty and Kathy left the house. We thought that Marty was praying for her. When they came in, Kathy stayed with him.

After a few minutes, Marty spoke, "Kathy, I believe it is about your bedtime. Could I have your bedtime prayer?"

"Yes."

"Lord, would you touch Kathy and heal her body and give her a good night of sleep. I pray in Jesus' name. Amen." He hugged her and said goodnight. She went to the bedroom with her mother.

When Elsie walked back in the room, Marty spoke again. "I don't know if God will heal her instantly or if it will be a gradual process. Don't take her off of any medication or stop any program until the doctors say that it is no longer necessary. Let me hear after the oncologist completes Kathy's test. Don't tell anyone I prayed for Kathy. At best, I am only God's delivery boy."

After the appointment, Dick called Marty. "The doctor says that something has changed!"

Good reports came with each visit for the next few months. Then a new spot appeared! All were devastated. Marty and I hit an emotional low. We had no clue as to what was happening.

Dr. Ludwig DeWitz, a professor of Old Testament and Hebrew at Columbia Theological Seminary, was visiting in our home. As the three of us walked home from a meeting, Dr. DeWitz asked us, "What is wrong with you two? You were always so full of life and positive in your attitudes. What is happening that could make such a change in you?"

We held back no details. We sat in the living room. Dr. DeWitz was quiet, and then he got down on his knees. When he rose, he said, "Marty, God says that you are getting the glory."

Marty spoke. "I don't understand how I could be getting any glory. I was scared. I told Dick and Elsie not to tell anyone that I had prayed for Kathy."

Marty phoned Elsie. Their Koinonia group had been meeting. There had been excitement over Kathy's good reports. In response to questions, they shared that Marty had prayed and laid his hands on her for healing.

Dr. DeWitz, Marty, and I dropped down to our knees, asked God's forgiveness, and prayed that He alone would receive glory for what He had done.

On the next scheduled visit to the oncologist at the University of Virginia Medical School, Kathy's parents received great news. The spot that had increased in size was now closing! It would be final. Praise and thanksgiving rose to our Lord.

EPILOGUE

Twenty years later, Kathy graduated as president of her class at the nursing school at the Medical University of South Carolina. She is married to a great guy, David Fant. They are the parents of two children, David Jr. and Daniel Richard.

Kathy's father, Dick, and her brothers, Rick and Clark, are of national renown as competitive water-skiers. At the National Water Ski Championship finals over the last twenty years, Dick, Rick, and Clark have been stars in slalom, jumping, tricks, and overall competitions. We praise God for this athletic ability and the hours of discipline and commitment required in achieving these goals.

Martin (Marty) Harkey is a graduate of the University of Virginia (BEE), Columbia Theological Seminary (MDiv and ThM) and San Francisco Theological Seminary (STD).

> I assure you, most solemnly I tell you, if anyone stead-fastly believes in Me, he will himself be able to do the things that I do; and he will do even greater things than these, because I go to the Father. And I will do [I Myself will grant] whatever you ask in My Name [as presenting

all that I AM], so that the Father may be glorified and extolled in (through) the Son. [Yes] I will grant [I Myself will do for you] whatever you shall ask in My Name [as presenting all that I AM].

—John 14:12–14

Chapter 12
LOSS OF BALANCE

*L*ORD, IF *I could gain wisdom like Solomon, I could speak it into many of the situations that I frequently encounter. Many people, even Christians, do not study Your Word very often. Why, Lord, sometimes days pass that I do not open Your Book and meditate upon its truth! I want You to lead me and guide me more intimately. I ask You to give me a hunger for Your Word.*

For the next six months, I proceeded to devour the Book of Proverbs. I lived in the book. I ignored all other teaching God had provided on His scrumptious platter, the Bible.

The day arrived for my annual trip to Rich's Department Store, North Decatur Branch, Decatur, Georgia. In their book department, Bibles were annually marked at half the original price. Since I am of Scotch-Irish descent, I enjoy a bargain.

As I studied and made notes in each yearly purchase, I realized I spent more time in the Word. I would star verses that spoke to my life situation at the time. I underlined and wrote triggered thoughts in the margins. Many of these Bibles I saved; other copies I shared with friends and acquaintances who welcomed a more up-to-date translation.

This particular day, with a joyful heart I made my way down Interstate 85 from Anderson to Atlanta. My plans were to locate and purchase a new Bible and to mosey through Rich's and Davison's Department Stores to see if there were any items within my price range I could not leave behind. This was always a relaxing day. I usually stopped at a public phone and dialed the number of friends out of my past.

I took the I-285 exit and followed it to the North Decatur Mall. Rich's would be the first stop. Avoiding the enticement of many attractive items in the departments through which I strolled, I arrived in my favorite book department.

After careful examination of many versions of God's Word, I decided to buy a Harper Study Bible (Revised Standard Version). My choice was of fine leather, good quality paper, and had excellent study notes. I was pleased with my decision.

Handing my credit card to the clerk, I waited to sign.

After two additional hours of feasting my eyes on all the new and improved products offered in several stores, two early Christmas gifts were purchased and my day of shopping was complete.

The drive home did not seem long. I listened to classical music presented by the Philadelphia Philharmonic Orchestra. A light dinner was easy to prepare, and the kitchen was quickly made tidy. My husband left for a YMCA board meeting. Our younger son, still a teenager, was playing basketball with friends. In my mind, there was no question about what I would do to fill my evening.

Finding the most comfortable chair in the house, I sat down and opened my new Bible. My mind had difficulty believing what my eyes told me was true. No Proverbs! From Psalm 137 to Ecclesiastes 7 was missing—a whole section! In shock, I examined the remainder of the Book. Every other page was in order.

A year later, I walked up to the Rich's book department manager. I shared with her what had happened regarding my purchase. Very graciously she repeated Rich's promise of satisfaction to every customer. "Bring it back. We will give you another Bible."

"No thank you," I replied. "I would not take anything for that Bible." I told her how for six months I had excessively studied the Book of Proverbs at the exclusion of all other books. I needed correction!

Think of the possibility of a meticulous book assembler failing to include a section of the Bible he or she is charged to compile! Or ponder the odds of my selecting that particular Bible! (The manager insisted that this was the first time she had run into this problem.) All this to move me out of Proverbs into other parts of the Word. We serve a God of balance! Remember, I had prayed, "Lead me, Lord, in all of life, even the small choices, and give me a hunger for your Word." He does answer prayer!

> But my lord has wisdom like the wisdom of the angel of God—to know all things that are on the earth.
>
> —2 SAMUEL 14:20

> Behold, You desire truth in the inner being; make me therefore to know wisdom in my inmost heart.
>
> —PSALM 51:6

Chapter 13
A SURPRISING EXPERIENCE

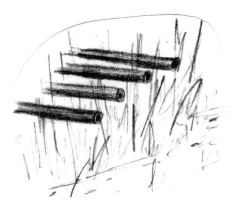

I N THE SPRING of 1989, we walked into a precarious situation. Four long-barrel guns were pointed at us! Marty and a younger minister were asked by the presbytery's mission committee to host a group of fourteen representatives on a trip to the Central American country of Guatemala.

The primary purpose in making this trip was to offer both encouragement and resources for various phases of mission projects that would benefit Mayan tribes scattered throughout the country. Four of our group had traveled to Guatemala a year earlier in order to become familiar with the splendid projects underway by the Protestant church of Guatemala.

We appreciated this part of the world, the beauty seen in deep, clear blue lakes and mountains with a background of very clear skies by day, wrapped most evenings with beautiful sunsets. Small volcanoes circled the country. We watched several craters exploding into the night sky—memorable!

The citrus fruit and bananas were tree-ripened and full of flavor. Cashew nuts hung from the trees in very hard, kidney-shaped hulls. They were both a visual and gastronomic treat to North Americans as well as residents.

One captivating work involved a village of ninety Mayan Indian widows and their children. A few years earlier, the widows' husbands and teenage sons were made to stand before a firing squad. It seems these innocent people earlier had been caught in crossfire, as they were forced by men with guns to feed an opposing rebel faction. This prior action angered the group that took their lives.

The remaining widows and children were extremely poor. Our partnership aided the Guatemalan church to serve them. The women and children were being taught to read and write, to develop and market their crafts, as well as health habits and sanitation. An elderly farmer was hired and moved into the area to teach them how to prepare the soil on the hillside and to plant and harvest nourishing crops. Seeds were developed in the United States to flourish in the soil composition of this country. The message of God's love revealed in Jesus Christ was faithfully proclaimed to them.

On this day, our destination was to be the area where the widows were then located. Marty, a take-charge guy, had to set himself aside in Huehuetenango in the company of a huge Coke. This was due to a twenty-four hour case of Montezuma's revenge. Assuring him of our prayers, the decision was made by the group to stay on schedule with the local host. We would make the trip without him. With his blessing, we boarded the van. We enjoyed singing and conversation as we viewed the country and the activities taking place in the many small villages.

At one village, we witnessed the unusual recruitment of students for military life. They were asked to vacate the school bus and line up beside it. If they were strong in appearance and had good teeth, they were escorted to the service vehicles as new recruits. Their families would have to be told where they had gone.

When we neared the area close to where the widows now lived, there was a high level of anticipation in all of us. Those of us who had met the widows the previous year looked forward to renewing acquaintances with these people.

A young Mayan girl balancing a loaded basket on her head met us down by the road to lead us up the mountain trail to the place where we were to meet with the group. We followed her up the winding path taking us through the woods and between large rocks. I noticed that at each fork in the trail, we were taking the path to the right, and then we followed a slightly winding path along the ridge of the mountain. Eventually we arrived in an open area where a cement block building had been constructed to be a gathering place.

After an informative and inspiring time spent with the widows, the time arrived for us to be on our way. A widow told us in a kind way that no one could lead us down the mountain to the van. No explanation was given. There seemed to be some reluctance to take on the task. Did they know something we did not know? I quickly volunteered to take on the job. I told them I had grown up in the West Virginia hills where my dad had been a pastor. "No problem. I can do it," I said. "Let's go!" All were agreeable.

I moved to the front of our group confident it would be only a matter of time and the group would be comfortably back on the bus. We walked the ridge, made the left turns at each fork, and arrived at the path that would lead us down the mountain. As we came out of the woods, I was delighted to see our van looking like a matchbox toy on the side of the road at the foot of the mountain. Though an adult, I was skipping like a kid ahead of the group. Nearer the bottom third of the mountain, the path had been cut through tall grass. As we neared the tall grass, my eyes spotted the barrels of four guns being pointed in our direction. My first thought was, if the guns are fired at me, the others could possibly get away. A second thought was directed toward the Lord: "Help! What must I do?"

Immediately, three thoughts became indelible in my mind:

- Remove your ring. (It was set with glistening, inexpensive Guatemalan marcasite stone.)
- Continue without fear.
- Wait until you are even with the guns, then wave vigorously, smile, and say, "Buenos días!"

I followed these instructions carefully. It was like watching a movie as we slowly moved down the sloping path and approached the tall grass where the gunmen had stationed themselves to our right. Mustering a smile, I said, "Buenos días." The guns were lowered! (Could it be that we were not the only ones that the gunmen saw manifested before them?)

The gunmen allowed us to pass and continue down the path to our van. Our driver, knowing nothing of the experience, suggested that we relax and he would serve us soft drinks from a cooler. Several voices said, "Could we move on down the road a few miles before we take our break?"

Four months later, at the Global Mission Conference of our church in the mountains of North Carolina, one of the Guatemalans who had been with us on the trip and the young minister who had grown up in that culture shared feelings from this experience. Both men were fluent in Spanish and had an excellent grasp of the thinking and emotions of these border people. They sought me out and said, "We were just talking about the guns put on us that day, and we still shiver when we think about the experience. Because of the poverty, some have been killed just for their shoes!

If your six-foot two-inch tall Marty had been leading us down that mountain, he would have been shot without hesitation."

I reckon those young men did not know what to do with a crazy Caucasian woman who, with guns pointed at her, could still smile at them and say, "Buenos días."

Our Lord's ways are certainly higher than our ways, and His peace incomprehensible. Praise Him that the rebels are no longer a threat in this fine country.

> A man's mind plans his way, but the Lord directs his steps and makes them sure.
>
> —PROVERBS 16:9

Chapter 14
LIVINGSTON

O N A TRIP to Guatemala, we visited the detailed relief map in Guatemala City, which had been created for their government officials. Volcanoes, mountains, lakes, valleys, cities, and roads were featured. It was a popular tourist attraction spread like a coverlet over a city block. My eyes were drawn to an isolated town on the northeastern shore. Livingston was the name. It was the title chosen by the earliest settlers, who had come from Africa by way of a shipwreck. I was interested!

"They must have heard of David Livingstone, the Scotch missionary and explorer," I said.

Our guide responded, "As far as we know, they are a closed society and do not know of Livingstone's faith. Many years ago, a slave ship went down off the coast. The only survivors were women and children. Those early settlers developed into an ingrown matriarchal society. Male children were taught very little about the language; strangers were not welcome."

On Sunday we scattered to different outpost churches, in order to participate in the Sunday services. At one church, we dropped off a music team.

On the porch of the church, we met the minister. In less than three minutes of conversation, he mentioned the town that had caught our attention earlier. He volunteered this information: "I grew up in Livingston and moved away as a young man. I became a Christian after I left home. My mother and sister still live there. I am the only black minister in the Evangelical[1] Christian Church of Guatemala."

Back in the States and several years later, our friend Rowena Lyle invited us to dinner; she wanted us to meet a family from a Wycliffe team of translators whose name had been given to our church's mission committee in response to a request from us. We were a mission-minded church and desired to expand beyond our present mission support. Rowena's husband, Bill, had been chairman of this committee. This family had first become acquainted with the challenging work of the Wycliffe translators' team members as they worshiped with some of these families at the international church in Mexico City. Rowena and Bill became excited over the work being done by these people.

During the mealtime conversation, we asked this visitor to tell us about the project presently receiving their undivided attention. "We have labored for a long time and recently completed our last assigned task. At present, we believe we are being led to work with the African people who speak the Carib language. We think an important key is found in a town known as Livingston, located in Guatemala. It is a closed matriarchal society. We are praying we will meet someone whom the women town leaders trust."

Marty and I looked at each other.

---

1 In Guatemala, the term *evangelical church* means that it is a Protestant church.

In our excitement, we both spoke at once.

"On our second trip to Guatemala, we met a minister." I kept silent for Marty to continue: "His sister and mother live in Livingston. We'll get in touch with the church leaders and ask for his address. He told us he was the only black minister among the Protestants in the country. He said to us, 'I became a Christian after leaving Livingston.'"

The information was promptly sent to church leaders in Guatemala, and quickly we were given the young minister's name and passed it on to the translator.

Years passed, and we had moved to another state. One day, the phone rang. We were surprised to hear a recognizable voice say: "I am in the States for a few weeks for my daughter's graduation from nursing school. She is with me, and we are coming in your direction on our way to visit family before we go back to Guatemala. Could we meet you two for a visit and lunch?"

We were delighted and were both able to be free. We met with the translator and his daughter, and they followed us to a restaurant located near the interstate they were traveling. We were delighted to renew the acquaintance.

They shared with us that the minister of color was glad to make contact with his family in Livingston. Furthermore, his mother and sister had worked with our Wycliffe friend and the other members of the Wycliffe team, as well as others in Belize and Honduras who spoke their dialect. Thanks to their work, Livingston now has some Christian residents!

Our Wycliffe friend asked us to join them in prayer that many more people would share the joy of knowing Jesus as Lord. Our casual meeting had been used by the Lord to help the team that translated portions of the Scriptures into a language these people could understand. God is awesome!

Together we praised a God who beautifully plans His work! He is the greatest economist of all time. He wastes nothing!

> Roll your works upon the Lord [commit and trust them wholly to Him; He will cause your thoughts to become agreeable to His will, and] so shall your plans be established and succeed.
>
> —PROVERBS 16:3

Chapter 15
THE STRANGER'S SEARCH

THE INTERIOR OF the new-to-us, Spanish-style manse had been attractively redecorated by the previous homeowners. The surrounding property, including an orange grove, needed attention. Our congregation had purchased the land for future expansion. The overgrown property gave the appearance of an abandoned movie set. A couple of the church kids suggested it looked like a ghost house.

For several weeks, many helpful church members put forth strenuous physical effort as they used scythes and mowers on the high grass and pruning shears on the overgrown shrubbery. With the grass mowed, we noted many sandspur plants. Children were an important part of our church family; we were concerned about the potential consequences of the sharp spurs on the tender feet of the children.

Not into spraying poisons, I decided this job would be easy to handle through other means. It was exciting to do a small share of the many new jobs to be done. A floppy hat provided me shade from the Florida sun. Blue jeans and a long sleeve shirt, plus tennis shoes, had me ready for the job. Picking up a couple of containers, the choice was made of where to start. I rejoiced at how easily the sandspur plants lifted out of the sand—quite a contrast from digging grass from the clay of Georgia and the Carolinas.

The containers were filled, emptied, and refilled for several hours. Pausing, I wiped my brow and the perspiration trickling down my face. Glancing toward the church, I noticed a couple looking around the buildings. This action did not seem unusual, for it was tourist season. Many times tourists would stop and visit as they looked around a public building.

I observed the couple walking toward me. An unusual thought entered into my mind. It was like an internal voice speaking to me. It was clear and kind. "Tell the lady coming toward you she is forgiven."

Not accustomed to receiving a direct word from the Lord, I said, "Lord, I have never seen this woman before. If this is You speaking, please confirm it."

As the couple drew near, I could see her face. Her eyes were red and tears were streaming down her cheeks. The man had his arm around her, offering comfort. Confirmation?

The lady spoke. "We are from Ohio. We are traveling Florida in search of something. We were on the East Coast last week and did not find it. We felt led to this particular church. We did not find it easily." She paused a moment, then continued. "Do you know anything about the church next door?"

"Yes, I am the pastor's wife. It is a very friendly church. We worship the living God, who manifests Himself as Father, Son, and Holy Spirit. We appreciate each other and pray our lives will bring praise to the Lord. I do not know what it is that you are seeking, but when I saw you walking toward me, God said, 'Tell the lady walking toward you she is forgiven!'"

There was a moment of surprise. She grabbed the man, and a catharsis followed. After she regained her composure, she explained, "It has to be God speaking through her; she has never seen me before. God has forgiven me! Take me back to Ohio. I am going to be fine!"

As they walked across the grounds toward their car, I prayed, "Lord, this is a new experience for me. If you can help others through me, I would count it a privilege."

> He, being full of [merciful] compassion, forgave their iniquity and destroyed them not; yes, many a time He turned His anger away and did not stir up all His wrath and indignation. For He [earnestly] remembered that they were but flesh, a wind that goes and does not return.
>
> —PSALM 78:38

Chapter 16
HOT DOG BUDDY

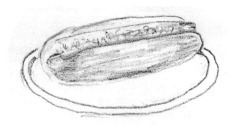

WAYLAND, A PRESBYTERIAN College graduate, had completed his masters of science degree in planning at Florida State University. Until his new bride completed her graduate degree one semester later, he was working at temporary jobs. Full-time positions were not readily available for qualified young males. In America, we were trying to correct a great wrong that had been allowed for generations.

He had been to many promising interviews, only to learn that he was well qualified but affirmative action guidelines called for a female or a minority person to give the company needed balance. He knew that managers were trying to be fair, but it left him without a challenging position.

As his mom, I, too, hurt for him. I knew that he needed to live his own life. I was helpless to advise him. My spirit was restless. I found peace only on my knees as I chose the path of fervent prayer to our heavenly Father.

Wayland attended a lecture in the field of his choice. The speaker was a CEO in this field and a man of great reputation. His presentation had excited Wayland with new, more efficient approaches to old problems. He had been given much to think about and would have appreciated further conversation with the speaker. Others were seeking the speaker's audience. Our son drifted back to his apartment.

It was a week later. He walked past the Foot-Long Hot Dog Shop. "I couldn't resist" he said. "I turned back and walked through the door. I placed my order and then began people-watching while I waited. Each person was getting pleasure from their special 'dogs' lavished with all the trimmings—onions, mustard, chili sauce, and fine-grated slaw."

The excellent speaker that he had heard a week earlier was sitting in a booth by himself. He was obviously enjoying his hot dog!

Wayland said, "I felt a nudging and then a thought: 'Ask him if you can sit with him to eat your hot dog.'" He tossed the thought. It would be too presumptuous. He paid for his hot dog and walked out of the door.

He sensed a second nudging, and the thought returned. He recognized that it was the Lord speaking to him. "You do want to pursue this subject with him, don't you?"

He turned around and opened the door and walked to the booth where the speaker was sitting. He introduced himself and told him that he had attended his lecture a week before and appreciated the practical concepts that he had learned from the presentation. "I liked what I heard. Do you have time for me to join you?"

The gentleman was very gracious as he asked him to sit down. Wayland asked questions to gain the depth of the speaker's suppositions. It was a positive experience. When he felt that he had taken enough of his time, he thanked him and departed.

A few months later, Wayland called a potential employer in one of Florida's major cities and asked him if he had read his job application. "I've had a six-month grant offered to me, but first I would like to investigate a permanent position."

"Young man, I have a stack of over one hundred resumes on my desk applying for our opening, and I already have a number of highly qualified candidates. If you have any kind of job offer, take it."

Wayland's wife, Beth, whispered to him, "Ask him if he would mind looking at your resume and telling you in what areas you fall short in qualifying for the position." Wayland asked him and said that it would help him in his search for a long-term position.

"I will do that for you," the employer said. There was a long silence, and then the voice of the employer was heard. "You are well qualified. I will need time to check on your references. I will be back in touch."

One week later, he was called by the employer and invited for an interview. The day after the interview he was offered the job. One year later, he learned that his list of references had not been contacted. Only one call had been made, and it was to his "hot dog buddy," who held the top position in the field at the state level.

The response of the "hot dog buddy" had been, "If you can get Wayland Harkey, you should hire him immediately!"

Our heavenly Father has foreknowledge of our individual futures. He has plans for each of us and longs for us to listen to His voice and seek His guidance.

> Yes, You are my Rock and my Fortress; therefore for
> Your name's sake lead me and guide me.
>
> —PSALM 31:3

> For this God is our God forever and ever; He will be
> our guide [even] until death.
>
> —PSALM 48:14

Chapter 17
SUNGLASSES

L EAVING ON VACATION before dawn the next day, our travel would take us across many states. Before exiting the city, we decided to refresh ourselves in the nearby Gulf of Mexico.

Marty and I had with us our only grandchild, Rob, a two year old, who had been experiencing febrile seizures. Doctors seemed to have no explanation for his situation. We had insisted his young parents bring him to us to give them a break from the constant observation and stress.

It was a hot June day following several stormy days. The beaches were peppered with sunbathers; the water was heavily salted with swimmers. It brought to mind Fourth of July pictures in *Life* magazine of Coney Island or Jones Beach in New York City. You could observe people as far as the eye had visibility. The strong winds and waves had scattered cockleshells like a carpet. The normally sandy bottom was covered with them. Huge breakers made the restless Gulf look like the Atlantic Ocean. As they jumped the waves, or were knocked down by their force, tourists and local folk were full of laughter.

A tremendous wave struck Marty and Rob. The wave took with it Marty's prescription sunglasses. At this time, sunglasses to be clipped over prescription glasses were limited in their availability. One-hour replacement glasses were still a dream. The choice was gone as fast as it was presented. "It was either Rob or the glasses. I had no choice; the waves had such force," Marty volunteered.

Noting our distress, a young woman on the beach raised her voice above the other voices around us, "What happened?" We did not know she had been watching us. I waded in from waist-deep water to explain our dilemma.

"I'm sorry," she said in a sympathetic manner, "This surf will sweep away articles faster than you can imagine. Only a miracle could bring up those glasses in that Gulf."

"I'm going to pray for that miracle," I responded. Dodging the moving people, I walked to the edge of the water. "Lord, please help us find those glasses."

Side-stepping people, I walked approximately thirty feet into waist-deep water. Something touched the side of my foot. I stood still, and the next wave caused it to hit my foot again. I sensed it was the arm of the sunglasses tapping my foot. I reached into the stirred-up, sandy water. It was the glasses, and they were not even scratched, despite the large wave action upon people and shells. Amazed, I dropped my head, knowing that God had truly answered prayer.

The young woman kept watching us. She heard me scream with joy as I called to Marty. She saw me pull the glasses out of the Gulf much farther out than the area in which he had lost them. She screamed, and a crowd gathered around her.

"That balding man holding the young child lost his prescription sunglasses as the waves knocked him down. His wife told me she was going to ask God to help her find them, and He did!"

God loves you as much as He loves me. Sometimes He does not answer affirmatively. When He does not, I trust Him. Eventually,

I am open to His peace. He is all-knowing and does what is best. He truly cares.

In 2001, Rob graduated from Davidson College and is currently enrolled in architectural school.

Do not fret or have any anxiety about anything, but in every circumstance and in everything, by prayer and petition (definite requests), with thanksgiving, continue to make your wants known to God.

—PHILIPPIANS 4:6

Chapter 18
THE MESSAGE

W ITHIN A CONGREGATION where my husband served as pastor some years ago, God brought together a group of eight young women who were full of His love and open to growth in His likeness. They were intelligent, caring, nonjudgmental, and able to keep confidences. We studied the Bible and read widely. We felt the freedom to express any thought or feeling and still feel accepted. We spent time each week in prayer for the needs of the church family, the community, our nation, and the world.

All ran smoothly in the prayer and discussion gatherings until one of the members, with permission from the rest of us, invited a lady to come and speak to the group. She was a member in good standing in another church. Attractive and winsome, she took me by surprise. Shocking me, she peeled off statements contrary to anything that I had ever read or been taught. She said that every believer could have a prayer language! I could listen no longer. I understood this to mean tongues, and I had heard what that could do to a congregation. It was terribly divisive! We had heard that when this movement broke out in a congregation, members set themselves up as more spiritual than other Christians. Furthermore, they did not worship decently and in order, like our part of the body of Christ.

Wondering if I was being judgmental, I paused. Was it I who was full of pride and not open?

The prayer group left. I rushed to my husband's office and repeated what I had heard.

Marty responded to my anxiety. "We have got to do something! This could cause trouble."

Mirroring the uproar within me and the distress in his own being, the two of us rushed to the speaker's address, as listed in the phone book.

After she politely invited us to enter, we registered our alarm at what she had voiced to our prayer group members, and then asked her never to repeat those words to them again. (This was out of character for both of us!) She answered us calmly and patiently, saying she did not want to cause any problem for us. She promised not to visit the prayer group again.

Time passed. I thought all was well. The ladies' prayer group continued to be a good experience as we met weekly discussing the Scriptures, sharing insights that we had gained, and praying for those with pressing needs—until Marty called me one afternoon and asked me if I would come to his office.

Present were the members of our prayer group. Marty asked one of them to repeat to me what she had said to him prior to my arrival.

She spoke, "I feel that you are controlling my thinking and restraining what I hear!"

I was surprised and hurt. Could this be true?

My private time with the Lord increased.

One day, as I was in prayer before the Lord, into my mind arose the thought, "How do you know I did not send your speaker?" It was spoken in great patience and love. I knew the statement did not originate with me.

We continued to meet once a week. I had little to say.

At our next meeting, the friend who had confronted me in Marty's office said she needed to share something that had happened to her. She told us she was cleaning her kitchen and singing. She did not understand the language or recognize the tune of the song. A thought came into her mind to call Carlos, an exchange student from Mexico, and ask him if he could tell her what she was singing. She obeyed. She called to Carlos and asked him to come to the kitchen for a minute. She continued to sing.

"Mom, you said you could not speak Spanish. You are singing in Spanish. I can tell you what you said." (Carlos had never heard the song prior to this experience.) He quoted to her the words she had sung. "Mama, you are talking to the 'Big Father,' not your father or an important person on Earth."

The next day she was sharing with her once-a-week maid the occurrence of the previous day. The maid answered her by saying, "For a year, I have prayed to God to give you this gift. I knew it would bless your life."

Within months, others of our group were blessed. They said when they did not know how to pray about a situation, they asked the Spirit of God to pray through their new prayer language. I began to wonder, "Lord, is this a gift You want to use through me? Help me, Lord, to be concerned about what You want instead of what others think of me."

Some time later, while alone in prayer, I uttered a word that for me had no meaning. Later, other words followed. I began writing the words phonetically as they came into my mind. One word was repeated on several occasions.

Possessing curiosity, I asked the Lord if this was a known language in use today. He answered me in an unusual way.

I made a trip to a food facility to pick up some chicken. The place bustled with customers. Not only were tables full, but the line was long for pick-ups of carry out orders. My eyes were drawn to an attractive young waitress. As she gracefully moved past me, I caught my breath as I read her last name, which was clearly printed on her tag. It was the same word I had repeated and written phonetically in my prayer language! Shocked, I paid for my chicken and left.

Operating in new territory, it took two weeks for me to gather the courage to return to the establishment. Entering, I scanned the place. The attractive waitress was not around. I waited. It was early and not a busy time. Recognizing the manager, I walked up to him and asked if he would identify the pretty, olive-skinned girl who had been working for him two weeks earlier.

"No problem! She is from Iran and is a student at our nearby college." I thanked him and left, knowing my prayer language is Persian!

The next Christmas, a Jewish couple and their two children arrived at our home. They were a part of a Christmas International House, a program for students from overseas attending colleges and universities in America. They were provided food, housing, and entertainment during the Christmas break. It was an opportunity for them to experience a unique two weeks in another part of the United States from the area they had chosen to study. This couple had selected our city on the word of close friends of theirs and good Jewish friends of ours. Their friends had encouraged them to duplicate the experience they had relished a year earlier.

This year we encouraged another local church to take charge. Their committee decided to care for the students in the homes of several congregations. We were asked to keep this couple for three days, including Christmas.

To make them welcome, I had displayed a menorah given to my dad and passed to me at his death. We had located candles for it. Expressing delight, the wife asked if it would be possible for them to have a Hanukkah service. They asked if we would we be present to worship God with them. This took place, and we appreciated the service.

Later, they were polite and volunteered to attend a Christian service, which Marty led.

Not long after their arrival, God impressed on me these words: "You will give her a message from Me."

I replied, "Lord, if this is You speaking, You will have to confirm it."

The next day, she shared about her life with me. At the age of seventeen, to avoid religious persecution, she and her family walked from Iran to Israel, leaving all of their possessions behind.

She continued, "My husband's position pays our bills. Our primary calling is to work with Russian Jews one night a week. These people arrive in our country knowing nothing of Judaism, except to annually identify them by raising the Star of David. We teach them faith in one transcendent God who has revealed himself to Abraham, Moses, and the Hebrew prophets and by a religious life according to the Scriptures."

As she spoke, I prayed silently, "Lord, I want to give her Your message, but I am afraid I will make a fool of myself."

The last day of their stay had arrived. I had said nothing.

The phone rang. The new host family was on the line. They had developed a plumbing problem and could not take the guests. "Would it be possible your family to keep them longer?" the hostess asked.

"Yes, we would be happy to have them."

The next day, I took her shopping. She was interested in a book in her husband's field of interest. I bought her choice and added an excellent local cookbook, *Carolina Cuisine*.

Parking my car in the garage, a question entered my mind. I spoke, "If I said something to you, could you tell me if it is Persian?"

"Yes, of course I still remember the language."

I opened my mouth and words began to flow. She was obviously surprised.

"Where did you study Persian?"

"I haven't."

"I don't understand; you are speaking to me in Persian!"

"Have you heard of Pentecost?"

"Yes."

"Do you know what you said to me?"

"No."

She seemed alarmed. Opening the car door, she said, "I need to tell my husband what you said!"

As she was leaving, God gave me another word for her, this one in English. "Tell her to let the words spoken drop into her subconscious mind. At a time in the future, I will bring them to recall."

She rushed into the house.

I did not feel a release to ask her what I had spoken. Later in prayer in my spirit, I felt I knew. What do you think God said to her?

> Now, brethren, if I come to you speaking in [unknown] tongues, how shall I make it to your advantage unless I speak to you either in revelation (disclosure of God's will to man) in knowledge or in prophecy or in instruction?
>
> —1 CORINTHIANS 14:6

The foot of the cross is level. This gift does not make you a better Christian than any other believer. Many of the most Christ-like individuals I have known did not have this gift, but they had others more valuable. They were full of overflowing love, peace, and joy and could preach, teach, minister, and speak with wisdom. God is love, and He revealed His love to mankind by the supreme sacrifice for us—His only Son, Jesus.

Chapter 19
THE MOVE

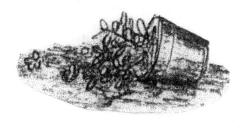

IT WAS A Monday morning in January, and an unusual cold wave had moved into upstate South Carolina. The thermometer registered eleven degrees above zero. The cold wave brought ice and snow.

This was moving day! It was soul wrenching to realize we would not be experiencing frequent contact with this congregation of people, whom we loved like family. In addition, we would be leaving our only daughter and son-in-law.

After the commercial movers had packed all of the contents of our home and left our driveway, my husband, Marty, friends, and I spent hours cleaning the house, which was filled with over nine years of memories. We wanted the place to sparkle!

Friends helped us load the last of sixty plants into the two cars that we would drive south. Our canoe was secured to the top of the car Marty planned to drive. As an afterthought, and to my embarrassment, frugal Marty secured two bags of cow manure to the top of the car I would be driving. Thoughts of the overloaded and uncouth contents in the prominent car featured in *Grapes of Wrath* rose to the forefront of my memory. Members of our new congregation would be at the manse to meet us when we arrived.

Would they want to rethink their decision to call my husband to be their new pastor?

Seventeen years had elapsed since we left this church in Florida to enter seminary, and in that time Marty had served two pastorates. Now we were on our way back to St. Petersburg.

We felt God was calling us to return to the church we helped to charter. Many happy memories were associated with that time in our lives, yet leaving Anderson was like giving up a limb from our bodies. We had become a part of a close-knit community.

The city limits of Anderson had not been reached before I flashed my lights to get Marty's attention. I needed to stop! One of my car doors was ajar. I opened the door to close it securely, when I heard something fall to the ground. I got out of the car and retrieved my favorite African violet. When the pot hit the ground, all the blooms were beheaded. I picked it up and said, "I know how you feel."

We drove and drove. The car radio informed us we had not succeeded in traveling beyond the freezing weather. Too weary to drive further, we were approaching the exit to Valdosta, Georgia. Tired as we were, we had all sixty indoor plants to unload and move into a motel room. Some of the plants were large and had lived with us for years. What would we do? Marty, driving behind my car, asked this question of the Lord.

Into his thoughts these words were spoken: "Nearly every gas station you pass has a grease rack. The room containing the grease rack is a heated garage. Stop and ask the attendant if you could park your car overnight for a small fee."

The next exit led to a Sheraton Motel with a gas station to each side. First, we checked to make sure space was available at the motel. Assured of a room, Marty approached the manager of the first station. Explaining our predicament, he offered three dollars to park his car.

"I will leave before eight o'clock in the morning."

"Fine," was the response.

Marty was excited as he pulled his car into the motel parking space close to mine.

"You go up to the room; I will bring the overnight bag as soon as I settle your car in the second station grease rack."

Several moments later he arrived with a smile on his face.

"We are all set! The canoe is safe, and the plants will not freeze."

I interrupted, "Unfortunately for me, I will be continuing to carry my top load of fertilizer."

Before receiving this knowledge in his thoughts, Marty commented, "I had never thought of the grease rack as a heated garage."

It surprised us that almighty God cared about our little concerns enough to intervene in our lives.

When we arrived in the Pasadena area of St. Petersburg, the members who welcomed us expressed immediate delight as they observed the fertilizer. "You are down-to-Earth people with whom we can relate!" they commented.

Expect the Lord in your life! When have you recognized Him? Even though He may have broken through before as He spoke to the circumstances of your life, were you open to listen to Him? You will never be bored! You will recognize Him by His character, His love, and His caring. His corrections are firm, yet they are couched in love. If we will give Him His way in our lives while we live on Earth, when we go to be with Him, it will be like another step in our walk.

> Time and chance happen to them all.
> —ECCLESIASTES 9:10, RSV

> My lord has wisdom like the wisdom of the angel of God—to know all things that are on the earth.
> —2 SAMUEL 14:20

Chapter 20
SECOND CHANCE FOR MARY

L ORD, MAKE ME *fearless, and use me for your glory.* I believe my prayer brought Mary to me. She was in her late teens or early twenties, slender, with clear skin, brunette hair, and dark brown eyes. She was clothed in slightly wrinkled play clothes and wore torn, dirty tennis shoes. As she moved about the meeting room at a large inner city church, she seemed ill at ease, recognizing no one. When she came toward me I welcomed her and invited her to sit with me.

She whispered in my ear, "My name is Mary. Take me home with you. I am hungry!" I told her that I would see that she was fed at the close of the study. Midway through the meeting, she slipped out of the room.

When my commitments were met, I looked for her. In the chapel, stretched out and asleep on a pew, I found her. I touched her and she sat up. She willingly accompanied me to my home.

The drive was in silence, except for one request. She wanted me to stop at a Christian bookstore and rent an Amy Grant music video. We made the stop and she located the video. I paid.

Arriving at my home, she refused food and asked to watch the video. From the kitchen, I observed her seated on the floor. As she watched, she began to sing with Amy. I was amazed! She knew all the words and music. Her voice was beautiful, especially when she sang in harmony with Amy.

Marty arrived, and I ran outside to meet him and to tell him about our guest.

At dinner, Mary ate and ate and then asked where she could sleep. We opened our guest room door. She threw her body on the bed and begged us not to ever let her go.

"Lord, what do we do? Please guide us," we prayed.

The next morning the phone rang. My friend Arlene called saying that she had an extra seat at her table for the citywide President's Wives Luncheon. Featuring top-notch Christian speakers, this event was always a sellout. It was an accomplishment to get an available seat. Elizabeth Dole had been our previous year's keynote speaker. Billy and Ruth Graham's daughter, Ann Graham Lotz, who presented the main address at the World Evangelism Conference in Switzerland, was the featured speaker for this year.

Lying in bed awake, Mary heard me call the news to Marty. Mary's voice shattered my excitement. "I want that ticket," she said. After breakfast, I reluctantly told Mary she could have my ticket.

Marty and I decided that I would take her home. On the way, I told her that I would provide transportation for her on the day of the luncheon. I wanted to know whether or not she had changed her mind about using the ticket.

I followed her directions to her home on an inner-city back alley. She lived in a concrete unit that stood alone. It contained one room with a bath.

I asked her if she had something she could wear to the dinner. She asked me to wait and she would show me. She retrieved a bag of cast-off clothing from under her bed. A piece at a time, she began pulling the wrinkled garments out of the bag. I saw nothing that I felt would protect her from negative attention. I suggested we go to a nearby consignment shop.

"No, I'll wear this one!" It was a well-worn dress that had once been white. She assured me that she had an iron available and would make it look good.

"What about shoes?" I asked. She was confident she had shoes.

On my way home, I stopped at a branch post office for stamps. At the door, I ran into my friend Beverly, who had taken me as her guest the first year that I attended this annual event. She asked if I would be attending this year. I told her that Mary would be going in my place.

"Let me pick you up, and we will go for Mary. And hopefully there will be two ladies who will not show and there will be seats for us." It was worth a try.

Beverly arrived in a new car. Mary seemed pale when we picked her up. She was wearing the white dress, nicely ironed, and the same dirty, torn white tennis shoes she was wearing when I met her. We tried to welcome her but had to bite our tongues concerning the shoes.

As we parked, Mary grabbed for the door, opened it, and began vomiting. She walked a few steps and repeated the nasty action. When it happened a third time, I could stand it no longer.

"We are taking you home." I said. In one voice, a firm "no" rose from Mary and Beverly. I tossed a flash prayer toward heaven.

"I am uncomfortable, Lord, but You be the guide in this situation."

We made it through the Hilton Hotel lobby to the registration table. Beverly and I were granted permission to escort Mary to the table located near the front where Arlene was waiting. Mary broke away from us and began to finger the magnificent floral display at the center of the stage. We were able to quietly encourage her to go with us to meet her table hostess.

In a second phone conversation, I had warned Arlene that Mary would be present in my place. Arlene and I both were apprehensive about the situation and held similar opinions, but we had no other choice. Perhaps the Lord was working on us in areas of pride and image.

About a half-hour later, Beverly and I were notified there was a seat for each of us. Two seats, and unbelievably, a third seat, were the only vacant seats in this, the largest banquet room. Approaching the front table, I told Mary that we had an extra seat at our table. All seven beautifully groomed ladies spoke: "She's ours!" Blessed with their attitude, Beverly and I could relax and enjoy the occasion.

Not long after the luncheon, an appointment was made for her with a highly qualified counselor. By phone, Mary agreed to be ready to go at my arrival.

Appointment day arrived; parking to the side of the alley in front of her home, my ears were pierced with extremely high decibels of music blasting from her radio. A second sound was like a fan in need of attention. The noises created a cacophony.

Several times I knocked at her door, and finally, in desperation I called her name and reached in the window to lift one of the heavy, blowing drapes. The room was empty!

Disappointed, I turned to leave and met an elderly woman walking toward me. "Have you seen Mary?" I asked.

"I don't pay her no mind. She is always getting in and out of cars!"

My thought was, *She must be a prostitute! Could drugs have led her in this direction?*

Opening the car door and placing the key in the ignition, I

started the motor. After fastening the seat belt, I put the car in drive. I moved forward realizing I had to make contact with the counselor concerning Mary.

The thought was quickly erased as my car was struck from behind. It was quite a jar. I looked in my rearview mirror to see an angry man who was shaking his fist at me. I knew it had to be Mary's pimp!

Realizing I was in danger, I prayed, "Help, Lord!" His car pulled up beside mine and lightly side-swiped me. I turned quickly into a six-lane boulevard, drove about two blocks, and made a quick left turn. My pursuer was caught off guard and lacked time to follow me, for the light instantly changed to red.

The counselor's office was only five blocks ahead of my location. I drove hurriedly, parked, and rushed to her door. She was ready for us and was very gracious. Telling her about the situation, I shared the little I knew about Mary, including her assertion that her father was a physician, and the counselor affirmed my fear of a possible drug/prostitution ring. "It is very dangerous for you and Mary. Go to the police!"

I agreed. The station was just a few blocks away from where Mary lived. When I arrived, I spoke to a detective privately. I told him where Mary was staying and that she wanted to be free. He said he would take the information and contact the person whom she named as her father, although he doubted that this was true. If he was her dad and would pay for her rehabilitation, we promised to break her out.

"Don't go near her again!" the detective warned. "This is the kind of situation that turns up bodies. Let us take over now." As I drove home, I felt peace in my heart. The Lord was still in charge!

Several months later we moved to another state. Some time after our move, a picture postcard from another country was forwarded to our new address.

> Thanks for all you did! I am now teaching English in this faraway land.
>
> LOVE, MARY

I prayed, "Lord, like Mary Magdalene, I pray Mary will stay clean, give You all the credit, and learn to love You extravagantly!"

> For God did not send the Son into the world in order to judge (to reject, to condemn, to pass sentence on) the world, but that the world might find salvation and be made safe and sound through Him.
>
> —JOHN 3:17

Chapter 21
LITTLE LEAGUE COACH

RETURNING FROM OUR summer break, the two of us were traveling south on I-85. At the time, home was St. Petersburg, Florida. We had crossed the Florida state line when the needle on the gas gauge dropped dangerously low.

At the next exit, my husband chose a gas station and pulled into a line to wait for a pump. Seated in the car, you could observe a number of little league baseball players milling around, each with a cold drink, crackers, or candy in hand. The atmosphere these boys created was one of celebration. Many young dads were mingling among them. As one youngster drew near to our car, the following words were visible on his cap: Anderson, S.C. Underneath that it said S.C. State Champs.

Marty had last served a congregation in Anderson. We had moved to Florida a year earlier. Lively conversation developed. These young ones were on their way to St. Petersburg, Florida, for the regional little league baseball playoffs.

They would be playing the next day at the Gulfport field. The time was given. In my mind, I made plans to be present for their game.

On my way to the location and the specified diamond, there was excitement for these kids and their dads. I took a seat on one of the benches. The game had begun. After observing a couple of innings, my thought was, "Something is not right." Turning to the lady seated next to me, I said, "The South Carolina boys are not playing with heart. They had to be good to win their state championship. I arrived a few minutes ago. Has something occurred to affect their play?"

"You don't know? Their coach's heart stopped. They have taken him in an ambulance to a hospital. The players do not know whether he is dead or alive."

"Did you hear the name of the hospital?"

"No, but I heard it was close by."

Palms of Pasadena was the nearest hospital, and they did have a cardiac intensive care unit. I rushed to the car to drive to the hospital.

Taking the elevator to the floor where the cardiac unit was located, I raced down the hallway and encountered a number of young men. Approaching one, I asked, "Is the Anderson, South Carolina, coach here?"

When the young man said yes, I spoke, "We moved here a year ago from Anderson. The church where my husband is pastor is located one mile from this hospital. Our manse has extra bedrooms and baths. We have a second car. These we will make available for any family members who may desire to be close by."

One young man said, "We were wondering what we would do. We all have jobs, and we need to return to Anderson; yet we could not think of leaving our friend without support."

Handing him a piece of paper with my name and phone number,

I went to the church. The young coach's name must be placed on the church's prayer chain. The father with whom I had a conversation at the hospital had thanked me and shared that they would be praying, along with many relatives and friends. Local prayer chains in other churches would join the chorus.

"Lord, if the coach can bless You and others, would you give him more time?"

Pat, the coach's wife, flew into the Tampa International Airport. Her close friend arrived a few days later. Staying at our home at night, their days were spent at the hospital. Their presence was a blessing to Dewey.

Two weeks later and much improved, Coach Dewey Freeman responded to the excellent care of the local heart specialists and God's healing touch. Joyfully, he was released. Marty was driving the four of us to the Tampa International Airport. We were crossing the Bay on the Howard Franklin Bridge. God spoke to my spirit: "Tell Dewey that his players have been worshiping him instead of Me."

Calling his name, I dared to speak. I related God's message to him.

In confirmation and humble spirit he said, "You are right. I will talk to them."

Without realizing it, many of us who are "people persons" allow others to praise us for what God has done through us. This can become worship. When it does, it grieves the only One deserving worship.

Lord, make us sensitive to accept appreciation, but help us realize when it is crossing the line. May I accept correction as beautifully as did Dewey. Thank You for returning this father to his sons and players and more of the sport they all love.

I will praise the name of God with a song and will magnify Him with thanksgiving.

—PSALM 69:30

Chapter 22
ANY HORSES IN HEAVEN?

THE WINDING ROAD and the trailers to each side of it had grown old.

I knocked on the door of a trailer where two elderly sisters lived. They could no longer climb on a city bus to take care of their weekly grocery purchases. They had accepted my offer of a ride to the bank to cash their Social Security checks and to a store of their choice for basic supplies. It would hopefully be an exciting outing for them.

Their supermarket of choice was located in South Pasadena, approximately two miles from the Gulf beaches on Florida's west coast. On our arrival at the store, the sisters each took a cart. With total abandon and joyful countenances, they directed their carts toward the produce section. To their delight, they sighted their favorite childhood foods—parsnips and red raspberries.

At this time, I left after telling them, "Take your time, and I will meet you at the front of the store." Having made an earlier trip to shop for our family, I found a comfortable bench facing the entrance and took a seat alone. As I awaited them, little could I have fathomed the experience that would become etched in my memory.

The air-conditioning was a comfortable change from the August heat, and the soft semi-classical music in the background was pleasing. Being appreciative of people, I began watching those who entered the store. It was entertainment for me. I studied the characteristics of their faces, their emotions reflected in expression and voice. I noted the carriage of each one. Perhaps unfairly, my imagination had a ball. Lacking genuine knowledge, I guessed what each life encompassed.

And then he was standing there—a tall, elderly man who could have qualified for a football lineman in his youth. Like a gun, he pointed his white cane at the electric doors in front of me. The double door would open, but he did not move toward it. He aimed his cane again. He repeated this action three times. On his fourth attempt, I was moved by the evident confusion expressed on his face. I jumped up and rushed through the open entrance to offer my help. Accepting my tender by reaching his hand in the direction of my voice, he said, "My name is Thomas, and loss of vision is new to me. I had a stroke. I was just released from the hospital down the street. The doctors told me I almost died."

"Were you ready?" I could not believe what had come out of my mouth and was spoken to a total stranger. It was like a tape from my childhood being played again through me. (My dad, as a young pastor, had often asked a similar question of others in my presence.)

There was silence between us.

"What do you mean when you ask if I am ready?"

"You know, we will all meet our Maker one day. As human beings, we will never be good enough to reach God. Most of us do not murder or steal or take advantage of others for our benefit; but at times, we all harbor negative attitudes and emotions toward others. Sometimes we say offending, indelible words, or fail to take advantage of an opportunity to administer good deeds. The Bible tells us this is sin, which makes a gulf between us and the

Father. The good news is, He has provided the way to Himself through His Son, God in the flesh, the perfect sacrifice for sin. He has bridged the gap between man and Himself. We have to accept the gift. In other words, have you received Jesus as Lord of your life?"

He hung on every word and obviously wanted to talk further. Together, we walked to the bench. He sat down beside me. A moment of silence followed, and then he began to thoughtfully speak.

"When I was a young boy, I had a horse that I loved better than anything on Earth. I would ride, pet, feed, and groom her. I knew she loved me. One day, my dad hurried into the house and said, 'Son, your horse is dying. Run quickly to the barn!' I tore out of the door, and it was as if my body had wings as I raced down the path to the stable. As I got to the gate of her stall, I called her name. Ever so slightly, she raised her weak head—and then she was gone!

"Dad came into the stall and soon left; he realized I needed to be alone. I was devastated. For weeks I would not talk to anyone. I did not want to eat; I did not want to live! A few days later, I overheard Mom and Dad talking about my depression. Dad took me to talk with our minister. He asked me about my horse. I told him what I have told you. I could tell his mind was on other things. I paused in my story, then he quickly told me to forget my horse!

"'You will never see it again,' he said. For over seventy years, I have hated a God who does not love horses!"

From me these words came: "Thomas, I believe if you will invite Jesus to be Lord of your life and allow His Spirit to live in you, you will see your horse again."

"You do?" He leaned toward me, obviously wanting to hear more. I continued, "In the beginning God created everything,

95

including humans and animals. A person has a human spirit, and animals have animal spirits. Ecclesiastes 3:19 says, 'For people and animals share the same fate' (NLT). In Genesis 9:5, God's covenant with Noah says, 'For your lifeblood, I will surely require an accounting. I will demand an accounting from every animal. And from each man, too' (NIV). We are talking about a God who loves and wants only the best for men, women, and children, and animals in whom He can delight."

"You are a Catholic?"

"No, I answered, but I am a Christian. I came to know Jesus as my Lord in a Protestant church."

"Where is your church?" Thomas continued his part of the conversation.

I gave him the name of the church my husband served as pastor. To our surprise, it was the same denomination of his childhood minister.

This encounter took place during the busy Florida tourist season, at a time when the church was packed every Sunday. If Thomas came, I missed him. But when I recall that day, I know Thomas did not miss the Lord. He is His man—ready!

> After that I saw heaven opened, and behold, a white horse [appeared]! The One Who was riding it is called Faithful (Trustworthy, Loyal, Incorruptible, Steady) and True, and He passes judgment and wages war in righteousness (holiness, justice, and uprightness).
> —Revelation 19:11

> The wolf and the lamb shall feed together, and the lion shall eat straw like the ox; and dust shall be the serpent's food. They shall not hurt or destroy in all My holy Mount [Zion], says the Lord.
> —Isaiah 65:25

Chapter 23
OLD YELLOW

I BELIEVE THAT YOU and I often write off, as luck or circumstance, God's intervention in our lives. On this day, I was confident that neither luck nor circumstance could apply to what happened.

I was driving "Old Yellow." She had sat for years under a carport on Florida's West Coast. A dear friend whose vision was now too poor to continue to drive owned this car. The car was clean, with low mileage, and had a good transmission. My friend's mechanic had made a very low offer for the car. She said to me, "You need a change of wheels. I will let you have her for what the mechanic offered." My husband and I talked the matter over and decided to go for it. I drove her for the next seven years.

This specific day, I had completed my errands and was heading home when I heard a loud noise. One of Old Yellow's tires had blown. I stopped and then slowly drove her, with tire flopping, to the curb on a side street. I got out and walked to the front door of the nearest house. The lady who answered my knock wanted to know who I was and where I lived. This tack surprised me, because I expected her to ask me what I wanted. I gave her my name and told her that I lived in the old Spanish house several blocks away.

Her first remark was, "I have admired that house for years. I have always wanted to tour it!" (Built in 1926, it was a landmark. It had been purchased for the land on which it stood by the church where my husband served as pastor.) I told her a tire on my car had blown and if she would let me use her phone to call AAA, I would make a date for a home tour within the week. She was delighted!

After contacting AAA, I waited only a short time for the arrival of the tow truck. The young man who was sent to help me felt he could change the tire and replace it with the spare tire. He said: "No need to pull her in." He tried and tried to loosen the rusty nuts and could not make them budge. He cursed the Lord in a loud voice. I heard myself say, "If you would ask Him to help you instead of cursing Him, I'll bet He would do it." He tried again. In my spirit I prayed, "Help him, Lord." The nuts began popping off almost as fast as he touched them. He looked shocked as he caught my eye. I was surprised too!

"Go worship Him next Sunday," I said, "but I'm moving to Georgia this weekend. Find a church home there, one where you sense His Presence." In my heart, I knew that he would follow the suggestion.

Your ways, Lord, are not our ways to lead a young man to Yourself. Your way is more exciting! Thank You!

> Seek, inquire of and for the Lord, and crave Him and His strength (His might and inflexibility to temptation); Seek and require His face and His presence [continually] evermore.
>
> —Psalm 105:4

> For everyone who keeps on asking receives; and he who keeps on seeking finds; and to him who keeps on knocking, [the door] will be opened.
>
> —Matthew 7:8

Chapter 24
CARJACKING

THE BRIDGE SPANNED Boca Ciega Bay on Florida's west coast. In order to proceed, the boat captain sounded his signal for the bridge attendant to open the gates! My car arrived as the bridge was opening.

Relaxing, I caught a glimpse of the V formation of pelicans flying overhead. The soft breeze was swaying the Robilena Palms with their large pinnate-shaped leaves. The feathery Pigmy Date Palms were fascinating as they added to the beautiful landscape. Full bloom oleander bushes provided bright color. Good FM music from the CD blended to make the break a joy.

As the barriers lifted, I turned the key in my ignition and began to move. Driving about three miles, I slowed down to a stop at a red light. Synchronized with the green light, a terrific blow was felt from contact with my rear bumper; the unexpected jar shocked me. A line of cars was revealed in my rear view mirror. There was no place to stop; I traveled to the next intersection, turned right, and located a place to pull over. The van behind me followed. I recall the windows of the van were tinted darkly. Until the driver opened the door, he was not visible.

As he stepped to the ground, I noted he was dressed in an unusual fashion. I remember thinking he looked like a prosperous Russian Cossack ready to go on stage. He sported a white-bloused shirt with a low-slung belt and bloused black pants. He wore spit polished military boots. I would later learn his dress was misleading.

As he walked toward me, there was time to quickly examine the back of my car. I tried to put him at ease. "My car has no serious damage. I see only a dent in the bumper. I won't press charges. I cannot fathom how you struck me with such force and did no more damage."

Totally naïve, I left my keys in the ignition and my pocketbook on the front seat. I expected him to thank me and be on his way. Instead, he walked rapidly toward me, shoved me aside, jumped into my car, and started the motor.

"My car is fine," I calmly persisted.

"I'm taking this car!" he shouted in a raucous voice.

"Then leave me my pocketbook; it is on the front seat beside you!" (My right hand was on the handle of the car door as I faced him.)

He thrust both his arms through the open window and grabbed me around my throat, his countenance contorted in an ugly expression.

He shouted, "You're going to die!" Strangely, I had no fear and noted his pearly white teeth looked surreal. The thought entered my mind, *I'm going to identify you by those teeth.* His grip began to tighten around my throat. (I do not believe he knew what he was doing.)

I softly uttered the Name above all names: JESUS.

The Name above all names broke his power. His hands dropped instantly. He raced my car motor and was gone! I stood alone in the company of his castoff car. I would later learn it, too, was stolen.

My knock brought no response at three of the nearby houses. At the fourth home, a couple stood together as the door opened. Feeling a little insecure about a stranger entering, they listened to me and said they would call the police for me. After they reached the police, they summoned me: "He wants to speak to you." Information was supplied and the receiver placed in the cradle. At this point, they told me I could call my husband.

Ten days later, the police called to say they had located my car. They asked me if I would come to make positive identification. My husband insisted on accompanying me. We traveled to the address given.

As we approached, we recognized the car and observed that it had been wrecked. Soon, two policemen and a detective arrived on the scene. The detective was a good friend and neighbor of ours; we knew we were in good hands.

In order to clarify details concerning the incident, one policeman began to ask for additional information concerning what had occurred. As I answered him to the best of my knowledge, three adorable children drew near to us. One of them spoke: "Another stolen car, and we know who it belongs to! He took us for a ride in it. Grandmother told us not to ever ride with him again. She said he got our mama pregnant!" A second child added, "We've just been to the store for chewing gum."

From these innocent kids, we learned the name of the young man and the fact that he lived nearby. They were reluctant to give us an address. I told them he had used force to take my car from me, as he threatened my life.

The oldest child started to speak, hesitated, pondered her thought, then said: "I don't believe Carl would have killed you."

I convinced them, I did not think he knew what he was doing when he stole the car. "He acted as if he were high on drugs and out of control. He needs help. If you really care about him, you will lead us to him. He probably does not even remember he told me I was going to die." They looked at each other, and one of them gave us the address of his aunt with whom he lived. The policeman sent a law officer to confirm the information. After a short period, the second policeman contacted us on his cell phone in order to verify the information the children had offered.

I asked the kids if they had seen a Bible in the car. One girl asked, "Did it have an X on the leather cover?"

"Do you mean a cross?"

She paused, then spoke: "I believe they do call that mark a cross. He brought it into our house and showed it to our mother."

The following week a detective called to ask for an appointment. He wanted to show me a mug pack. When he arrived and was seated, he opened the pack. To my dismay, not a single person was smiling. I was disappointed; identifying the offender by his pearly teeth would not be a possibility.

Silently I prayed, *Help me, Lord!* I looked again at the pack; one pair of eyes was familiar. "That one!"

"You're correct; his fingerprints were on your door handle and all over your mirrors, particularly the overhead one. We haven't located your license plate. We're holding the truck license placed on your car. We will pick him up and be back in touch with you."

A letter arrived, giving the court date. I answered the phone when it rang at 2:30 a.m. the day of the trial. A deep voice slowly spoke: "You know who this is, don't you?"

"I do and I am not interested in talking to you at this hour." I hung up; Marty unplugged the phones.

In court, we listened as charges for carjacking were read. The lawyer for the accused spoke: "Carl is only nineteen years old and this is his first offense. I say let him go!"

I stood. The lady next to me pulled my arm. "You are not going to testify are you? I would be scared!"

I stood up straight. The judge recognized me and asked if I was Mrs. Harkey.

"Yes, sir."

"Please speak."

"I believe Carl was high on drugs and out of his mind when this jacking occurred, but I do not think it would be wise to excuse him to repeat at will this negative behavior. He threatened my life as he closed his strong hands tightly around my throat. He took my car, pocketbook, and several purchases. He needs to be taught this is unacceptable behavior."

The state attorney asked the judge if he could speak.

"Yes, please do."

"This young man was accused of carjacking in Tampa, but no one showed to press charges."

The judge spoke again: "Mrs. Harkey, I agree with you. I will give him six months in prison and five years probation."

Later as I thought about this event an additional thought came to mind. Could Grandmother have been praying for her daughter and her grandchildren? If somehow, God would move in their situation, it could make all the difference in their world. Another thought followed: just possibly, Carl would open the Bible and read a life-changing word from John, or Peter, or Paul.

> The thief comes only in order to steal and kill and destroy. I came that they may have and enjoy life, and have it in abundance (to the full, till it overflows).
> —John 10:10

> And call on Me in the day of trouble; I will deliver you, and you shall honor and glorify Me.
> —Psalm 50:15

Chapter 25
IN YOUR LIFE EXPECT THE LORD!

Living in the valley of Virginia, at the age of six and a second grader, I accompanied my parents to the home of friends. Our hostess led me to their library. On the lower bookshelves I found puzzles, a View-Master with three-dimensional slides of exotic places, a toy truck, a doll, blocks, and many books. Some of the books were written for children.

As I turned the pages in a songbook, I found little stick people across the top of a page. Each stick figure had a circle head colored red, yellow, black, or white. It was a familiar song. I sang softly:

Jesus loves the little children of the world.
Red and yellow, black and white, they are precious in His sight.
Jesus loves the little children of the world.

My thought: "I want to be one of those children You love, Lord."

As a young woman, my desire was to walk with the Lord like Enoch of old...I told Him. Since that time, steps have been taken:

...some slowly

...some with apprehension

I have not arrived. It is with humility that I have shared a few portions of my walk in some of the preceding stories.

I read in the Gospel of John: "My sheep listen" (10:13) and "My sheep hear my voice" (10:27).

I said to the Lord, "I know I am one of Your sheep. I don't think I have recognized Your voice. I want to hear You with my mind and my heart."

I began pondering the subject: *How can I recognize the voice of God?*

Seeking the answer to my question, I studied the life of Jesus in the four gospels in the New Testament. I tried to understand His teachings. I spent hours with the Apostle Paul and his eighteen letters. Many times I covered all the Scripture in the Old and New Testaments. I worshiped with David's psalms.

I tried to surrender as much of myself as I know to as much of the Lord as I know. I asked Him what He would say to me at this time in my life. "Let me hear only your voice, Lord Jesus." I posed this request in 1973.

These words came into my thoughts: "My walk with you has required patience, but you have brought me much joy!"

It was the Lord! I would not make a statement like that about myself.

Into my mind came memories of times when I was sure I had tried His patience:

...running ahead of Him.

...doing things and saying, "Bless it, Lord; I did it for You." (Was it really for Him?)

...dragging my feet when there was something He obviously wanted to accomplish through me. (I was in bondage to what others thought of me.)

How do I recognize His voice? For me, it is in my thoughts. His thoughts offer fresh insights and wisdom. They are superior to my thoughts. Often they are encased in the fruit of the Spirit (Gal. 5:22). At times He offers comfort, encouragement, correction, a command, or guidance. He speaks to me through His Word. On other occasions, He speaks to me through other people. Sometimes a sermon from a pulpit is confirmed in my spirit that the word spoken was for me, and other times, He speaks through a child. Only our will and attention can limit His speaking to us and through us.

On one occasion, He gave me the name Nancy, then added, "She is praying for you." I knew which Nancy. I rushed to the phone and called her and asked her if she was praying for me. Filled with surprise, she asked, "How did you know?"

I responded, "My heart was heavy with the load of another person. With your prayer, my spirit became light. I found myself actually skipping down the long hall in our manse. God told me, He is teaching me how our prayers affect the lives of others." (From that moment, I would be more faithful in prayer for others.)

Into my mind, like a whirling winged seed floating to the earth from a maple tree, the name of a person is communicated by our Lord—one I must forgive, or one who has a deep need. When a name or situation comes to mind, I test it. Will the action I may take give God glory?

I remember one Christmas Eve when our oldest and his young wife were in Princeton, New Jersey, in graduate school. He was teaching his way through a doctoral program. We expected them in South Carolina on Christmas Day. At 3:00 a.m., I was awakened with the thought: "Pray for wisdom for these two young people."

They usually made good decisions. I could not put myself or the thought to sleep. I prayed. Next afternoon when they arrived, my first word to them was: "What were you doing at 3:00 a.m. that God would awaken me to pray for wisdom for you?"

Shocked by my question, Carolyn responded, "Luke had completed his examinations and papers, but would not leave for break until his students' work was carefully graded and placed on the school records. There had been a buildup of late nights to assure that all necessary work was accomplished. Completion of the task made necessary a later departure than anticipated. We traveled for hours. Feeling weary and agreeing that a break was needed, we took the next exit and parked in a motel parking lot to grab a few winks before continuing our journey home."

When God awakened me, they had aroused from sleep and were debating whether they should spend their last money on four hours of sleep in a motel room. Wisdom ruled and they walked into the motel. Did God spare their lives that night? I do not know, but He has taught me that a prayer requested by Him has to be important.

Become aware of His next invasion in your life. He knocks at the door of our hearts, and if we are open and will welcome Him, we will know His blessing!

> Be strong and let your heart take courage, all you who wait for and hope for and expect the Lord!
> —Psalm 31:24